# BUSINESS WRITING

Mary Dustan Turner, MA, designs and conducts communication courses in the UK, the US and Europe. A business writer and author of *Making Your Own Baby Food* (New York, 1976), she organised the consultancy Business Development International.

Robert Louis Abrahamson, PhD, provides training in communication through his consultancy, Verbatim, lectures in English and Management Studies for the University of Maryland's European Division and is a consultant technical writer for several international companies. He is the co-author and editor of the *Good English Manual* (London, 1987).

GW00702867

# TEACH YOURSELF

# BUSINESS
## *writing*

## Mary Dustan Turner
## &
## Robert Louis Abrahamson

Hodder & Stoughton
LONDON SYDNEY AUCKLAND

A CIP catalogue record for this book is
available from the British Library

ISBN 0-340-57399-6

First published 1993

Typeset by Rowland Phototypesetting Limited,
Bury St Edmunds, Suffolk.
Printed in Great Britain for the educational publishing
division of Hodder & Stoughton Limited, Mill Road, Dunton Green,
Sevenoaks, Kent

# CONTENTS

# PREFACE

This is a book that comes out of our experience as writers, trainers and editors. We have designed it for people in business who want to produce clearer writing in less time.

Many people fear writing because they 'cannot write well', but no one in business is asking you to be another Shakespeare. You just want to express facts and ideas clearly and coherently.

With this book you have a method for tackling any writing problem that comes across your desk. It gives you guidelines to the process of writing and includes templates and examples of types of business writing.

The book is divided into two sections. The first section leads you through the stages of producing a document, from first thinking about what needs to be said to preparing a final version. This section offers practical advice and contains exercises to help you practise the techniques shown.

The second section examines several kinds of business writing. For each kind of writing we offer a definition, a discussion of the purpose, a guide to what the document should contain and how it should be organised.

Obviously we cannot cover every conceivable variety of business writing, but you can apply the guidelines to any writing project.

Use this book as a manual. Refer to it when you want to produce a specific kind of writing for your job. We can, after all, only provide a start for you. Take our guidelines and adapt them to suit the needs of the particular task.

Our thanks are due to the many people who have helped us in this project. We would like to thank our students and all the people we have trained; it was through teaching that we developed the techniques presented in this book. We want to thank all those people in business who supplied us with ideas, advice and examples: in particular, Julian Barnard of Dawnstoke Computer Services Ltd, Ian and Judith Braid, David Clark of Clark Hollis Associates, Bill, John and Charles Cleghorn of Cleghorn Waring & Co (Pumps) Ltd, Peter George, Andrew Hunt, Roger Stubbs of ATP technical publishers, Neil Thornton, Patricia Trumps and Philip Veale. Our thanks to Judith Heneghan, the commissioning editor, and to Paul Smith, the present editor.

Our special thanks go to Juliet, Ian and Victoria.

# — INTRODUCTION —

Have you ever panicked when your boss has asked you for a report? Have you ever stared at a blank page, not knowing where to start? Have you ever had your draft sent back with the request that you rethink it?

This book will teach you the skills that professional writers use when they write. It will show you what they do before they begin to write so that the writing itself will be easier. It will teach you what techniques to use to make your writing convincing to your audience. And it will show you how to prepare your work for distribution once it is written.

In other words, this book is teaching you a system which is set out in easy, clear steps, with exercises to help you improve and examples to show you what the finished product ought to look like.

It will enable you to tackle any writing assignment that arrives on your desk. You will know how to get ready to write; you will know what to do to make the correct decisions about what form the writing should take; and you will be able to decide quickly what the finished product should look like.

Since no two writing tasks are the same, it is useful to master a system which you apply to each piece of writing that you do. This book will teach you that system.

# ——— A quick way to get started ———

Writers are made, not born. All successful writers – of novels, news stories, business proposals, plays or annual reports – go through a series of steps in the process of writing. The steps start long before the writer actually sits down to write. They start with the thinking the writer does before putting anything down on paper or on a computer screen.

The first thing any writer does, when given a writing assignment of any kind, is to look at what is available, at what is known about the subject and the people to whom it is directed. Start with the simple things, the things you know immediately about the subject, without doing any research. Make a list of them, working from the simple to the complex.

Ask yourself simple questions about what you would like to know if you were reading the piece. What would you need to know? Or, what would you like to know further about the subject? Do not worry at this point about whether or not you will include this in your final writing. Just jot things down. They probably will not make much sense right now, but that is all right. Just keep on listing things you know and things you would like to know.

When you finish take a look at the entire list. Do any of the items on the list duplicate each other, or relate to each other?

Begin to sort your list into sections, into naturally occurring divisions which seem logical to you. After you have done this, you should if possible leave it alone for an hour or a day.

But don't stop thinking about it. Think about it when you are doing something else. As you think, things you have forgotten about or that you have just realised are important to the subject will come into your head. Add them to the list.

Sort the list again, making further divisions. Can you begin to see the natural categories that the subject falls into? Once you do, you have the beginning of a plan for what you are going to write.

Naturally, the more you do this, the easier and faster it will become. This is what all professional writers do, no matter what topic they are writing about. Some people do it in their heads, others write the list on the backs of used envelopes, some put it on note cards and carry them around in their pocket to add to. But whatever system you use keep at it, keep adding to the list, re-arranging, sorting the categories further until you have the beginnings of an outline from which you will write. (We will talk about the next step and about setting up an outline on pages 31–41.)

This list is an example of the type of steps we will be showing you in this book. We will provide exercises which will test your newly acquired skills, and give you examples of specific types of business writing, such as answers to a letter of complaint, or a memorandum to your boss or a status report due each month.

## A step-by-step process

We will proceed through the book step by step so that with each chapter you will be adding to your skills. You can also use the book for reference by looking up the appropriate chapter when, say, you are faced with writing a proposal.

We see writing as a process which anyone can learn by following the step-by-step procedure. There is nothing mystical about it and people who are award-winning writers of best-selling fiction do not use a system any different in its basic form from this one. Each writer, of course, develops variations on it, but that is the joy of learning to write better.

If you follow the chapters and the step-by-step approach you will have taught yourself to produce clearer, more efficient business writing.

We hope you find this book useful. We have both spent many years teaching and training people in this system so we know that it works. We used it ourselves to write this book. And we have enjoyed writing it. We hope you will enjoy using it. Good luck.

## Misconceptions

Before we begin, here are some helpful background hints from one professional to another about things writers know but will not tell you.

We all hold certain misconceptions about the things that we write in a professional capacity. Many of these misconceptions arise because, having put our ideas, our careers and our egos on display, we think that what we have written deserves everyone's attention, if not everyone's applause. We anticipate that our readers are just waiting to read our writing. Such a view distorts the whole writing process and is responsible for much of the feeble and embarrassing writing found in business today. Other misconceptions about writing come from the ways in which we have been trained to regard writing while we were in school.

We need to eliminate as many misconceptions as possible to view our own professional writing with objectivity, learning to become our own best critic, our own best editor. Obviously, this change of attitude does not happen overnight.

**It takes time to view our professional writing disinterestedly.**

## *My report will be read like a novel*

Almost never is a professional document of any kind read from beginning to end like a novel. Instead it is *used*. It is used by the reader to check on certain facts, to carry out an action, to ascertain particular decisions or opinions or to help in influencing a decision. Think of the way *you* use business letters, memorandums or reports.

If, for instance, you work in the accounts department of a city council, when the consultants' proposal for the city centre comes in with a ban on vehicle traffic during working hours, you will not spend time reading the discussions of new traffic patterns but will turn directly to the section on costs.

## *People will be eager to read my writing*

Despite your hopes, your audience is not holding its professional breath waiting for what you have written; in fact, the audience is probably not looking forward to reading what you have written at all unless it promises an immediate profit. Picture your reader at a desk with a six-inch-high pile of similar documents that need to be read that day.

# My reader will know what I am writing about

The chances are that your audience is not a specialist in the subject, was not involved in the reasons behind the request for the document, may know little about the issues you are addressing and may not be willing to spend a lot of time trying to understand what you are writing about. Furthermore, you will not be around to answer any questions about issues that remain obscure, nor will there be anybody else the reader can turn to, especially if the document is being read on the train or at home.

All of this means that your document must stand on its own, containing – if only in a glossary and appendix – any additional information which the reader may need to follow what you are saying. The reader has little time and less energy to cope with the document into which you have poured so much of your energies and talent. The accountant, to return to our example, is actually much more concerned with balancing a budget than with your report itself.

# Only one person is going to read my document

Your audience may not remain the same. It is entirely possible that the audience may grow to include people and even other companies that you know nothing about. The document can be sent outside your company or to another department within your company. It may survive much longer than you anticipated, turning up years later in someone's files, to be incorporated into yet another document. Occasionally such things turn up on the front pages of a newspaper or on the evening news!

**Remember: your report or document, manual or software package, book or proposal must stand alone on its own merits, with its own language, now and at any point in the future when you may have long left the company.**

# Checklist of steps to complete a document

This checklist can be used for any report, documentation, proposal, memorandum or to a lesser extent even a letter. Depending on what you are writing you may omit some steps after *(i)* below.

*(a)*   Determine the purpose.
*(b)*   Identify the audience.
*(c)*   State in one sentence the main point you want to make.
*(d)*   Decide on a timetable for completion and distribution.
*(e)*   Research all appropriate and available data, documents, interviews, other reports, charts, illustrations, etc.
*(f)*   Adjust your main point.
*(g)*   Prepare a written outline in detail of what you want to say.
*(h)*   Write up a rough draft.
*(i)*   Edit and rewrite your draft as many times as necessary.
*(j)*   Check with your manager that the draft is acceptable.
*(k)*   Decide on the layout and design.
*(l)*   Choose the best method of duplication or publication.
*(m)*   Print it, or send it off to be printed.
*(n)*   Proof-read it carefully, checking and rechecking, revising if necessary.
*(o)*   Publish it.
*(p)*   Distribute it.
*(q)*   Publicise it if necessary.

---

In professional writing you must use formal standard English. You must pay attention to the proper use of grammar and punctuation. And what you turn out must look good and follow the conventions of your employer. You must write for an audience on the basis that it cannot return to you for clarification. Your document must then stand on its own. It should contain everything that the audience needs to understand it.

# PART I

# THE WRITING PROCESS

# 1
## —— PRE-WRITING ——

Pre-writing is a stage involving everything you do before you start to write. The majority of your time should be spent in pre-writing: in planning, gathering your information and thinking about your topic. Good pre-writing will save you time at the actual writing stage and will produce a more intelligent and easily understood document. Pre-writing consists of several stages:

*(a)* analysing the audience;
*(b)* determining purpose;
*(c)* considering tone;
*(d)* formulating the main point;
*(e)* gathering material;
*(f)* organising material.

## —— Audience ——

An understanding of your audience and its needs is essential in preparing any kind of business writing. If you fail to understand your audience, no matter how important your material, your document will not be as useful as it might be. Bear in mind that the letter, memorandum or report does not exist for *your* sake, but for the sake of the people who need to use it.

Each time you produce a piece of business writing, you are writing to a particular audience with different needs, individual characteristics and specific goals. Understanding your audience requires careful analysis and, most important, *imagination*. Picture your readers as clearly as you can, then put yourself in their place and try to see what they need and expect.

Obviously, if you write a memorandum each Monday morning to your manager on the progress made the week before (see **Progress reports**, pages 170–3), you do not need to spend much time analysing your audience. On the other hand, it is always better to take an extra bit of time to do it right than to be sorry later. Ask yourself what the manager needs to know and whether these needs are any different from last week's needs.

Longer pieces of writing, such as feasibility studies, proposals and reports, require extensive audience analysis to be fully effective. Letters, even routine letters, need some attention given – even if only for a minute or two – to the person you are addressing in the letter.

Start writing only when you know your audience. Take extra time to find out more about the individual people who will read the document. It will pay off in the long term. Pitch your tone, style, writing level and vocabulary (how technical the terminology can be) to the particular audience for whom you are writing.

**Analyse the audience, if only for a few minutes, every time you write something.**

Find out all you can about your readers in three important areas: education, personal characteristics and professional expertise and responsibility.

## *Education*

In analysing your readers' educational background, ask yourself these questions:

(a) What degrees, certificates or training do your readers have?

(b) Is their education/training in the area the document deals with?

(c) Is their education/training at a higher level than yours, a lower level or about the same?

(d) What languages do they use? Will they understand foreign terms? computer terms? technical language?

(e) Do your readers speak and read English as their first language? Is this British or American English?

---

A newly qualified engineer will know all the current terminology. But someone who received a degree 20 years ago and has spent the last 10 years in an upper management position may not use, or even know, the latest technical terms the new engineer may use automatically. A report from the engineer to the manager would do well, then, to include a glossary of terms. (See page 111.)

---

## Personal characteristics

It is sometimes difficult to find out many personal details about your readers, but anything helps. Personal relationships outside the office and family ties within any company can change attitudes and positions about anything and everything. If possible, be aware of your readers' personal idiosyncrasies and do not irritate unnecessarily.

For example, your reader may expect very formal, technical language, which you may feel to be inappropriately dense for the proposal you are putting together. (See pages 57–8.) You must nevertheless use the formal language the readers expect, or at least sit down and discuss the matter with your manager. Sometimes a writer may have to compromise in the interest of accommodating the reader. This is especially true for longer documents.

**Remember: the readers' needs, not yours, are paramount.**

# Professional role

Know the position within the company of the members of the audience. What is their relationship to you, the writer, or to the person commissioning the document? What is their professional relationship to each other? How crucial is the report you are preparing to their profession or status? Does it affect their future? Could your report jeopardise their job? Notice the way the writer of the memorandum on page 166 has carefully taken into account his readers' anxieties about new computers threatening their jobs.

# Levels of audience

Many writers make the false assumption that there will be only one level of reader. Even a quick consideration of the fate of your document once it leaves your hands will show how many different people may use it. It is always your responsibility as the writer to determine who makes up each level of audience. The audience may vary with each item you write.

**The primary audience** is made up of the person or persons to whom the document is most important. It may be the person who commissioned a report you are writing or the person who will put it to immediate use. It may be a member of the public or, in the case of a mass mailing, several thousand people living in a particular area. The primary audience may consist of your supervisor or a client you have never met or workers on the shop floor. It is crucial that you understand the needs of this audience since satisfying its needs is the primary purpose of whatever you are writing.

> The manager sitting in an office who *approves* your proposal does not read it in the same way as the shop supervisor who is actually *using* it to supplement a new technical procedure. In this case you should consider the shop supervisor the primary audience.

**The secondary audience** may be someone in the same organisation who will use the document for some less immediate purpose, such as adding its financial details to the budget or approving it for circulation. The secondary audience may also be your immediate boss, who reads and passes it on but who will not actually have to *use* it.

You may, for instance, write a sales report, with your supervisor as the primary audience. Your secondary audience may be someone in the accounts department who must look over your report to note and approve your expenses. Certain shorthand remarks that your supervisor will understand will not be clear to the accountant and should therefore be written out and explained.

**The tertiary audience** can be someone outside your organisation or someone whom you never actually knew about but who nevertheless makes use of your writing in some (often unforeseen) way. This tertiary audience may be someone who, years later, digs out your report to note your findings for some future project or who, living a foreign country, looks up your report to see how a certain project was carried out in your country. If your report relies too heavily on topical issues without explaining them, or on highly technical material, the tertiary audience will be lost.

Of course it is often difficult to know in advance who your tertiary audience may be, but take the time to check its possible existence and spare a thought to accommodate those people. One tertiary reader most people are aware of is the auditor from the tax office; another tertiary reader many people forget about is their manager's manager.

## *Checklist*

To help clarify the levels of user, ask yourself these questions:

1   (a)   Who make up your primary audience?
    (b)   What are they planning to do with your document, or because of it?
    (c)   Will they use the document every day or only once in a while?
    (d)   Will they read it once and make a decision based on it?
    (e)   Will they decide on its acceptance or rejection?

2   (a)   Do the people in your secondary audience use the document under similar conditions to those in your primary audience?

    *(b)*   What do these people expect from your document that differs from what your primary audience expects?

    *(c)*   Are they using it to run machinery, make a decision or carry out a procedure?

3  *(a)*   Will there be a tertiary audience?

    *(b)*   If you are writing an in-house memorandum or report, might it end up outside the company or away from the building with other readers?

    *(c)*   If you are writing a letter will it be passed to other people?

    *(d)*   How does the tertiary audience's use differ from the others' use?

    *(e)*   Do you know the people in the tertiary audience?

    *(f)*   Will you ever know them?

    *(g)*   If so, exactly what is your contact with them?

    *(h)*   Do you know enough to analyse their needs?

4  *(a)*   Do the people in each of these levels of audience know each other? see each other? speak over the telephone with each other?

Add your own considerations to this list.

**Think of yourself as the centre from which the report radiates to these different levels of audience.**

There is one further thing to consider about audience. Once you have identified your audience's needs, spend a minute anticipating any special problems that may arise between you and the audience. Do not avoid these difficulties, no matter how tempting it may be to do so. Face up to them, answer your audience's objections and add extra evidence or authority.

Suppose, for example, that what you are offering your audience involves dealing with a country which you know your audience prefers not to deal with. If you keep quiet, the audience may never know the deal involves that country, but there is always the chance that the audience *will* learn about it. Tell the audience what the deal involves and then convince the audience of the value of dealing with that country. If you cannot find sufficient arguments to convince your audience maybe your proposal needs to be reconsidered.

You will never be able to avoid office politics altogether: use them to your advantage.

**Remember: never begin to write until you have carefully analysed the audience as much as you can within the time allowed and with the information you have or are able to obtain.**

## Purpose

Writing for the business world requires you to be absolutely certain of your purpose so that you achieve what you want. Usually when you write anything in a business environment you are trying to make something happen. The business world is action-oriented. If a company does not hold its own in a market, it will stagnate and begin to lose the market. Your ultimate purpose, then, is to make sure your business continues.

Think about what is supposed to happen once your document has been read. Actions that can occur because of your writing include the following:

(a)   something may be bought, changed, accepted, adopted, adapted, restudied or rearranged;

(b)   your company may decide to allocate or spend money, or not to spend money;

(c)   staff may be hired, made redundant, reassigned or retrained;

(d)   equipment may be purchased, discarded, phased out or retooled.

Make sure you understand what actions are meant to follow from your writing. Use your audience analysis to understand your audience's requirements.

Do not forget that you are not writing for yourself or to show what you know about a given subject. You are writing because your readers need information, an analysis or an argument from you to conduct their business more effectively. You should set out that information in such a way that it can be used. Your audience wants to understand it, to accept that it is accurate and to locate it in your document easily. This is true whether you are analysing a procedure, proposing something new or arguing for a particular point.

**Purpose should be determined by what the audience wants and needs, and how that audience will use the information. It is also determined by what your company wants and needs. It is not determined by *your* own needs. Think of the audience and the company.**

## *Different purposes*

Sometimes it is difficult to understand the real purpose. The person asking for your writing may state one purpose, but there may be a hidden agenda. This is especially true with documents which will move up the executive chain to be read and discussed eventually at a board of directors' meeting.

If you are writing a proposal for a client your company may have one purpose in mind (to get the client to buy more services), while the client clearly has another (to improve business). This can make it tricky to decide on your purpose.

One way to make it easier to understand purpose is to consider its three different levels: short-term, medium-term and long-term. These three categories can apply both to your business and to your audience's.

Suppose you are a management consultant, writing a report to a new client about a new management strategy. Your short-term purpose might be to have the client approve the one new management strategy you are recommending in the report. Your medium-term purpose might be to have your client consider a six-month strategy campaign. Your long-term purpose might be to retain the client for at least five years. Of course, the underlying purpose, which applies to all businesses, is to make money and stay solvent. Many businesses will also have the ethical purpose of providing service to the public.

Your client's short-term purpose is to solve a single identified problem. The medium-term purpose may be to reorganise a department. The long-term purpose may be, first of all, to eliminate the need for hiring a management consultant at all. And, of course, the client's underlying purpose, like yours, is to remain in business and perhaps to be of service to the community.

## Functions of prose

It helps in determining your purpose to understand first what *function* you want your writing to perform. Still useful today are the categories which the Greek philosopher Aristotle formulated to classify the four functions of prose: **narration, description, exposition** (or **explanation**) and **argument**. Some writing performs only one of these functions, but quite often a piece of writing will fulfil two or more functions. You should try to determine which of these functions you are presenting in any given piece of writing. (Drama, fiction and poetry have different functions.)

It is important not to confuse these functions if you wish to produce clear prose – which is what business writing is about. One common fault in many documents is the attempt to *explain* how something works before having *described* what it is. Readers will have difficulty understanding an explanation without first knowing what the item looks like. Similarly many documents *argue* a case before *explaining* the situation. Again, it will be hard to follow an argument for purchasing a piece of equipment without first understanding how the equipment fits into the operation.

### Narration

A narration is an account of an event that informs us what happened, where and when it happened, how it happened and who was involved. People who want a narrative account of something, whether of a meeting or an incident, want to know **who, what, when** and **where**.

In the professional world only a few people are actually called upon to tell the *story* of something. Fire-fighters in their account of a fire must tell the story of how they arrived on the scene and put the fire out. Accident investigators must also recount the exact story of what happened: when did the accident take place? who was involved? where did it occur? Surgeons must write down the story of an operation from beginning to end: this narration then becomes a legal document in the hospital records. The report on Benslow Lane on pages 114–137 uses narration to recount the events that led to the present situation.

But in most professional writing narration is not called for, perhaps because it relies on chronological order – the most simplistic kind of organisation. Professional readers are usually looking for the *analysis* of an event or the *development* of an idea about an event, rather than a simple recounting of the event. As a general rule, do not use narration unless you are sure it is called for.

## Description

Description offers an image or representation of the appearance, nature or attributes of the thing described. You create this by citing the physical properties which will define the item for the readers. Such properties include *dimension, colour, weight, texture, material, density* and any other items of appearance important to the particular item or occasion.

It is important to *maintain the position* from which you view the item. Suppose you are describing a new piece of earth-moving equipment, a superior bulldozer, where do you start, where do you position yourself? If you decide your description will start with an inside view, you must not shift your position halfway through the description. (See pages 188–192 for further discussion of technical description.) If you are describing a physical space, such as a room, you need to establish for the reader the position from which you are viewing the space: if you are standing in the right-hand corner do not move to the left-hand corner. Stay where you are. Maintain the same *position*, or *point of view*, throughout the description.

Related to the point of view is the occasion for the description. An object or place can be described in many different ways depending on the circumstances. A description of a new kind of pen, for instance, will be different if addressed by the designer to the manufacturer, if addressed by the manufacturer to the distributor, or if addressed by the promotion department to teachers and students.

Descriptions are not just useful but necessary when you are working with equipment, a process, a building or a site. If you were a doctor writing about a wound, you would have to start with a detailed picture of the wound because the reader could not be expected to follow anything else about the wound without knowing what it looks like. When writing a user, repair or installation manual it is crucial to give your readers a description of what the machinery or object looks like before telling them what it does or what they should do or will be doing to it.

Some objects are so complex that describing them with just words is like describing a spiral staircase without moving your hands. Do not forget about using pictures in your description. Modern techniques for producing graphics are so sophisticated that there are few things that cannot be adequately illustrated. Often what would have taken three paragraphs to describe in words can be covered in one illustration. But do not let the picture do all the work; the picture is only a supplement, not a replacement. Do not omit a description in words.

## Exposition

In exposition you explain: you lay out the facts to make a point about something. For example, you can tell the reader how something functions, how it is used, why it does not work properly or how it went wrong. You can also explain when not to use it. You can make an assessment, a judgement or an explanation about it.

Exposition is the function of prose that most of us use most of the time in our professional lives. Any user manual, documentation, proposal or computer software program uses exposition. The manual required for the installation of a new piece of pumping equipment, the instructions on how to use specialised fire-fighting equipment, the manual on the functions of a laptop computer are all examples of exposition.

To write clear exposition we use various techniques, or patterns, such as comparison and contrast, definition, cause and effect, example and classification (these are discussed on pages 41–56).

## Argument

An argument presents a case to the reader, tries to change the reader's mind or urge the reader to take a particular course of action. Any argument must give the reader all the reasons why he or she should buy this, stop that, hire her, convict him or vote for this issue. An argument tries to *convince* the reader of the truth of validity of something or to *persuade* the reader to do something.

**When you present an argument make sure you have already
defined and described all necessary terms and parts of the
issue. Make sure you have explained before you argue.**

In a rational argument you should never resort to emotion (though, of
course, in sales pitches emotional arguments are the strongest – if not
entirely the fairest – weapons). Nor should you resort to threats: that is
bullying and only rarely is it effective in the long term.

Many people fall into the temptation of seeing only their own side of the
argument. If they do, their argument will come across as unfair, ill-
considered or even pig-headed. To be effective, you must recognise that
your position is not the only one. There is another side to the argument
and often your reader will be on the other side. If you can first consider
the other point of view and demolish it, and then follow on with your own
points, you will stand a much better chance of winning your argument.

---

If you argue that you should be allowed a month's holiday rather
than the fortnight you have previously taken, you must
recognise that your boss might have certain reasons for wanting
you away for only two weeks. Examine these reasons first and
show why they may not be valid. Only then present your
reasons for taking the longer holiday.

---

There is another advantage in attending to the arguments for the other
side. You show your reader that you have considered all points of view
and thus make your argument appear more reliable and impressive. This
is especially important when you are trying to persuade your reader to
spend large sums of money or adopt a new procedure.

One further problem with arguments is that it is often tempting to argue a
case when you are not asked to, especially when you are dealing with
material you feel strongly about or consider yourself an expert on. It is
also tempting sometimes to play it safe and avoid arguing. Be certain of
when your brief is simply to present your material and when it is to take
the further step of arguing what should be done about the material. It may
seem presumptuous to tell your reader what should be done when the
reader has not asked to be told (notice how you react to unsolicited sales

letters). On the other hand it may seem unprofessionally timid not to argue for a line of action if such an argument is expected.

**Argument should be the last of the prose functions you use.**

Once you have decided on the purpose of a particular piece of writing you need to spend a few minutes thinking about which of these functions you will use. Later you will do this step in seconds. (See also pages 54–6.)

---

# Tone

Tone can be defined as the attitude or personality that comes across in your writing. The tone you adopt can be very important to the effectiveness of your document since it often determines your reader's emotional response.

Although the content, the message, is what really counts, the tone plays an important part in the way your reader receives your message. Minutes that come across as chatty, for instance, will probably seem unprofessional; an invitation to a business breakfast that sounds like a letter from the bank will encourage few people to attend the breakfast. Spend some time at the pre-writing stage considering what sort of tone will be suitable for your document.

Your tone may be friendly, sympathetic, professional, officious, sarcastic, condescending or subservient. Your tone can be formal or informal, personal or impersonal. It is hard to dictate that certain tones are right or wrong (though it is almost always wrong to be sarcastic, arrogant or obsequious in business writing). It is probably better to speak about tone as appropriate or inappropriate.

All writing has tone. As an effective writer you must recognise the tone you want to establish and let it work for you. Give some thought to the emotion you feel (or pretend to feel) towards your reader or towards the situation the document is addressing; then determine how you are going to present this emotion.

By remaining aware of the emotions you have about the reader or the situation, you are in control of those emotions. If, for instance, you are angry and do not deal with your anger before you write, the anger will come out in the document. There may be the rare occasion when you decide anger would be appropriate, but even then refrain from writing in the heat of the moment. Your angry tone will be much more effective if you are thinking calmly about the anger and have brought it under control.

When we speak to other people, we convey tone not only through words but also through such non-verbal signals as voice and body language. In business writing too we convey tone through non-verbal signals such as the page lay-out, the type of print, the colour of ink and paper and the quality of paper. In this book, however, we are concerned only with the way words convey tone.

### Examples

Here is series of memorandums and letters John J. Jones, a manager in an accounts department, may have written in the course of a day. Notice the variety of tones.

1   The first 'memo' is a note written on the back of an envelope to Mr Jones's wife.

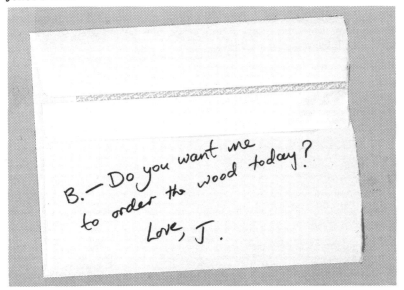

The lack of formality (no date, abbreviated name, personal pronouns, the unexplained use of 'wood', not to mention closing the note with 'love') conveys a tone of routine intimacy, the tone we would expect between people married for a number of years.

2    At the office, Mr Jones writes a little memo to the office manager on an office memorandum slip. Notice that while the tone is still informal the memorandum is less intimate. It conveys a tone of brisk, down-to-business efficiency. In circumstances like these, Mr Jones has to steer a delicate course between an overly familiar tone and one that treats George as merely an office menial.

The efficiency and informality appear in the absence of a date, in the initialled signature and in the single, direct sentence. The use of please and the handwriting help to soften the tone of the order and – at least so Mr Jones hopes – suggest that George is a fellow human being.

---

### M E M O

TO

FROM

DATE

*George, Would you please order more coffee for the machine today —J*

---

**3**   Getting ready for the forthcoming Board meeting, Mr Jones writes the following note to his assistant, Jane Reeves. This note also constitutes an order, but couches it in a different tone. Even though Mr Jones is the boss, his respectful tone shows that he values his assistant's opinion.

The question and the use of 'we' tell the assistant that Mr Jones respects her opinion. Again the lack of a date and the handwriting convey the informality used by people who work in the same office together and who are often writing in a rush. Mr Jones's initials, 'JJJ', signal again the professional relationship between the two people.

---

M E M O

TO          *Jane*

FROM

DATE     *Tuesday*

*Do you think we need the Marylux file for the meeting? — JJJ*

---

**4** When he looked through the Merrylux file, Mr Jones was dismayed to discover that the main report in the file had been submitted with numerous factual and grammatical errors and with many ambiguous and unclear sentences. It was obviously in no shape to put before the Board the next day. Here is the memorandum he wrote to Fred Anderson, the author of the report.

> Anderson — I have just gone over your Merrylux report and was appalled at how abysmally it was written. Didn't you learn anything from that training course we sent you on? You have until 2.00 tomorrow to make this report presentable. If I can't trust you with even a simple report like this, maybe I'd better think twice about keeping you in this department.

The use of the surname, the strong words ('appalled', 'abysmally'), the sarcastic question, the curt ultimatum and the threat in the final sentence all convey a tone of seething, angry displeasure (and perhaps panic at the thought of the impending Board meeting). This is not the kind of note anyone would want to receive.

**5** Luckily, being a responsible manager, Mr Jones thought twice before sending the memorandum and rewrote it. Fred Anderson was a newly hired employee with lots of promise. His writing was bad but with encouragement he would surely improve. In the second version Mr Jones swallowed his anger and sought to convey an encouraging tone.

# M E M O

TO      F. Anderson

FROM    JJJ  *John*

DATE    15 March 19--

Fred, I know how hard you worked on the Merrylux report, but I'd like you to go over it for me once more. It must go before the Board tomorrow and it must be as good as it can be. Please check the figures again. It would be worth showing the report to Monica or Jack to see if they spot any errors or if they think any sections might not be clear to members of the Board. I need the report back on my desk by 2.00 tomorrow so this will mean an all-out effort.

The acknowledgement of how much work Fred has already put into the report conveys a tone of calm encouragement. Notice too the way Mr Jones's tentative proposals suggesting what Fred should do convey a tone of confidence in Fred's abilities, and at the same time they clearly guide him in the right direction. This typed memorandum carries the tone of an official communication although the handwritten signature conveys a hint of informality from a colleague. This tone does not infect Fred with the panic Mr Jones is feeling. But it leaves him in no doubt that there is work to do.

**6**   Finally Mr Jones prepares a memorandum to the chairman of the Board giving formal notice of the presentation he and Jane Reeves will give at the meeting.

# MEMORANDUM

TO        F. B. Thorne, Chairman

FROM    J. J. Jones, Manager, Audit Department  J J J

DATE     17 March 19--

SUBJECT   Audit Report at Board Meeting

At the meeting of the Board on Thursday, 18 March 19--, Mrs J Reeves and I will present the findings of the Audit Department after its investigations into the Honeydew and the Merrylux accounts.  The presentation will need ten to fifteen minutes and, of course, we shall be pleased to answer questions.

The long first sentence, the initialling next to his name, the formal reference to 'Mrs J. Reeves', the actual date instead of 'tomorrow', 'the findings of the Audit Department' instead of 'our findings', the lack of any friendly or personal remarks, all indicate a formal style appropriate to an official statement, part of the ritual of participating in a formal Board meeting.

## *Choice of tone*

How can you determine what is the best tone for the kind of writing you are undertaking? Usually, with a little imagination and common sense, the choice of tone is obvious. You have to decide how you want to come across to your audience – a decision based more on business acumen or psychology than on writing skill. People in sales determine whether they are going to give their customer a hard or soft sell depending on how desperate they are to make a sale, how desperate the customer is to buy, what sort of competition exists, what sort of presentation the customer is expecting. Similarly you as a writer must determine your audience and purpose (see pages 9–15 and 15–21) and then decide the best way to come across on the page. Sometimes, however, the decision about tone is taken out of your hands. Tradition or company policy may dictate what tone is appropriate for certain kinds of writing, and then your job is simply to follow what is appropriate. In America, for instance, many business letters take on a hearty, friendly tone, or an earnest, sentimental tone, but unless your business is trying to promote itself as American in style, such a tone might not be right in a British context.

When you have to produce a kind of document you have not worked on before or when you are new to a company, it is a good idea to spend some time reading other documents of the same kind that the company has produced in the past. This will help you get a sense of the tone usually expected in these circumstances. But beware: these documents from the past may not be written in a tone appropriate for the present, especially if the economic or social culture has changed or if a new regime is trying to steer the company in a new direction.

---

**Hint:** Sometimes, as you are trying to write, you may find the words simply do not flow. You start and stop, you delete, you crumple and throw away paper. You look for any excuse to get out of doing the writing. Do not panic; all writers experience this sometimes. One way around the problem is to adjust your tone. If you lighten your tone or perhaps make it more straightforward, you may find yourself much more at ease with your reader and your writing will flow more quickly and accurately.

---

## *Adjusting the tone*

Because so much of the tone is conveyed through words, you may think that if you pay careful attention to the words you are using, you will get the tone right. This is true to a certain extent, and we will return to this idea in a minute, but there is a better, less self-conscious way to get your writing to sound the way you want it to.

Get a clear picture in your mind of the relationship between you and your reader or of the image you want to convey. The more vividly you can create these pictures and see yourself projecting the image you think is appropriate, the more readily will your writing express the tone you want. You do not need to worry about getting the tone right. It will come naturally and more smoothly than if you self-consciously try to construct the tone word by word.

There *is* a place, however, for consciously examining the relationship between your words and your tone, and that comes in editing your draft. (See also the chapter on **Style**, pages 56–62.) As you go through your draft, one of the things you should look for is whether you have consistently kept to the right tone. Be sensitive to the sound of your writing and catch those points where it goes wrong. Try reading it aloud and listening to the feeling conveyed in the words.

Use the following tips to help you be more sensitive and to give you an idea of how you can make adjustments to your tone.

### Personal pronouns can lighten the tone.

One of the simplest ways of lightening your tone and making it more personal is to use personal pronouns. Instead of,

*It is important that all forms reach this office by next Friday.*

try

*You should get your forms to us by next Friday.*

or

*We need your forms by next Friday.*

A manager writing a memorandum to all staff might say,

*The co-operation of all employees is necessary for this project.*

But the manager could seem more friendly and perhaps inspire more co-operation by saying,

*I need you all to co-operate on this project.*

or better yet,

*We all need to work together on this project.*

## Positive expressions can promote good will.

You can make all the difference to your tone by turning negative remarks into positive ones. Try to avoid words like 'failed', 'wrong', 'inadequate', and, especially, 'stupid'. Notice the hostility that comes across when you say,

*The parts your company sent us last time were the wrong size. Don't do this again.*

Perhaps on occasion you may want to be hostile, but if you feel a less unpleasant tone is called for say,

*We hope this next order will arrive well before the final delivery date.*

Be sure that your positive statements do not sound insincere; you can quickly lose your reader's confidence that way.

## Out-of-place apologies can damage your tone.

Be careful about apologising unnecessarily. Do not say you are sorry unless it was your fault in the first place. To say,

*I'm sorry your machinery broke down but unless we receive the parts by next week we shall have to place our order elsewhere.*

sounds begrudging, even vaguely threatening. It does not make the people with the broken machinery feel any better to hear you say you are sorry. Show your concern in actions, not in clichés like 'I'm sorry'.

## Technical language in the wrong place creates a pompous tone.

There are times when it is obviously necessary to use technical language, but if you use it in an inappropriate situation (see **Jargon** page 97), you may appear pompous and, possibly, antagonise your reader. The plumber who supplies a homeowner with a quotation using technical names for pipes and statistics about water flow will not gain that customer. The tone may come across as arrogant and the plumber will appear unconcerned about the homeowner's difficulties.

It works the other way too. If you avoid technical language when you should use it you may convey a relaxed, unprofessional tone that lowers your reader's confidence in you. The same plumber, when submitting an estimate to a building contractor, should provide accurate technical data or run the risk of losing the contract.

Again, it all comes back to knowing your audience and purpose.

### Exercise

Describe a single, stationary object from your professional field. First describe it in the tone of a professional speaking to another professional. Next describe it as though you were speaking to a non-specialist. Which was the harder description to write? Most good writers develop the ability to shift from one tone to another, depending on the occasion.

# Preparing an outline

The purpose of this section is to show you how to gather your facts, narrow your focus and prepare an outline from which you will be able to write quickly and efficiently exactly what you want to say.

Having analysed your audience and defined your purpose you need to complete the following steps before you write.

1  Think about your topic and what you already know about it.

2  Narrow the focus of the topic.

3  Gather all the facts and figures you need for your research.

4  Rethink the topic, narrowing the focus further.

**5**  State in one sentence the main point you want to make.

**6**  Prepare an outline of what you will write.

The steps listed above provide a process whereby you will finish up with an outline and be ready to start writing. Completing these steps is essential if you are going to have accurate information on which to formulate your main point and an organised structure that will create a coherent, concise piece of writing. This is true whether you are writing a simple one-page memorandum, a letter or a report of any kind, such as a feasibility study or a proposal.

Writing from an outline will increase your efficiency and accuracy. An outline sets out what you want to say *in the order* in which you want to say it. It saves an enormous amount of time at the writing stage by allowing you to concentrate on *how* you are saying something rather than on *what* you are going to say. And once you feel comfortable with it, after several tries, you will never again write without an outline.

Let's assume, for the purpose of an example we can use throughout this chapter, that your manager has said to you, 'Give me an eight- to ten-page report on the functioning of your office. I want to include it in the report I am writing for the Board of Directors about our department.'

That is all your manager has said to you. The rest is up to you. How do you proceed? What should you do first? What on earth are you going to do?

**If you are not sure about the purpose or objective of this report, go back to your manager for clarification rather than run the risk of writing what is not wanted.**

If you follow the step-by-step approach, you will create an outline from which you can sit down and write a logical, coherent, concise document in a much shorter time than you thought possible.

## Thinking

Sit down quietly, preferably at a time when you know you will have few interruptions, and simply *think* about the assignment you have been given. Jot down on a piece of paper with a pen or pencil (stay away from your word-processor or typewriter for the time being) everything that comes to mind when you say the word 'office'.

This is what is known as *brainstorming*. You just let your brain wander through the topic not organising or censoring it any way. As your mind wanders, write down whatever you think of. You can list your thoughts in columns down the page or you can follow another pattern some people find useful, called *'mind-mapping'*.

In *'mind-mapping'* you simply put the topic in a circle in the middle of the page and draw lines out from the circle with the topics at the ends of the lines. You can write one or two words for each topic or you can draw pictures or use symbols to build up visual associations. When you finish it looks rather like a spider with many legs going off in all directions.

## Exercise

Sit down now and carry out this thinking step, using the word 'water' before proceeding further with this chapter. It should take you about five minutes to do it. List the items you come up with either as branches of a tree or in columns.

Now try it for 'office'.

At the end of the first step, using the assignment to write about your office you might have a list something like the one on the next page.

atmosphere

light

air heating

cooling / air conditioning

function and purpose

   — mine ?

   — the company's

staff

   ~~trained~~

   untrained

   useful

   unnecessary

equipment

computers

printers

answerphone

furnishings

desk

chairs

carpets

curtains

work flow

   lunch breaks

   holidays

   ~~overtime~~

## Narrowing the focus

Focus on each of the items your brainstorming has produced, adding more detail, setting each one up at the top of a column. Go over them in your mind, perhaps eliminating some, moving others to another column. Think about which ones you would want to know about if you were one of the directors of the company.

You know from previous conversations that your manager's immediate concern is centred round the performance of the staff. He is not interested in the heating problems or in the furnishings. The equipment was new last year and you have just completed a report on how the equipment has functioned. You realise that his area of interest is the staff.

When you are sure that you have narrowed the subject to its critical areas you can begin to group them. Think about how to categorise the items. Put each detailed item in a category. Try to combine categories. Begin to organise the categories in order of importance. Which are really important? Which are not? Which ones can you obtain accurate information about in a reasonable length of time? Keep on sorting the items, narrowing the focus of your inquiries, changing the categories. Repeat as often as necessary, until you have two or three main topics you know are appropriate for your assignment.

## Gathering the facts

Having decided on two or three main topics you should now obtain as much information as you can about each one of them. Most of the information you need will probably be close to hand if you only look for it. Check through back files. Think about new sources of information. Seek them out. Write to them. Telephone them. Ask people you know either in the office or in other offices for specific information or the names of people who might be able to help you. Set up meetings with them and see what they can tell you. Make use of library resources such as indexes and bibliographies.

Use this same procedure for shorter documents, such as letters, adjusting it to the topic as needed.

## Rethinking the topic

Once you have amassed all your facts, statistics, quotations, charts, laboratory reports, etc. you must begin to sift out the information. If you have been alert you will have been doing this sifting all along but now you must begin to formulate just what it is you want to say about the subject.

Obviously you cannot write about every single thing you have discovered. Some of it is not important and some of it would probably best
be forgotten. Some facts may intrigue you but are not of crucial interest
or importance to your primary audience. (Remember to keep your
audience in mind at all times. See pages 9–15.)

To get back to our example: in the course of your research and your
rethinking you decide that the most important factor of all those listed is
the lack of training for the staff. You have recently hired two new people
and have realised that they are going to need additional training to bring
them up to the expectations of the company. You know that your
manager's report will include a large section dealing with the budget. You
decide you will use this opportunity to explain why it is important to have
money allocated for training all new people.

In addition, you have heard rumours among the experienced staff that
one of your competitors is offering training courses to its staff as an
incentive. You want to be sure you do not lose any good people.

Go back over the original list of items, rechecking your categories and
your priorities. Make sure the categories have not changed now that you
have more facts. Maybe one category you thought unimportant (e.g. the
telephone) is really more important than you thought since you have
noticed how urgently the new staff need training in using the telephone.

## Stating your main point

Write a sentence that summarises the single most important point you
want to get across in your document, the point you must get across if the
document is to succeed in its purpose and reach its audience. If you are
unable to put into one sentence the single most important point you are
trying to say you are not ready to outline. You should go back and rethink
your original list and check your facts.

In our example the main point would be something like,

> *We must provide more training for our staff or within the year we will lose*
> *our most valuable people to our competitor.*

Putting your thoughts into one coherent sentence is a check on how well you are doing. If you have done your research, thinking and classifying you will find it easy to write this sentence. If you are not ready you will have to do further brainstorming or re-examine your priorities.

**If at any point you have trouble go back over the steps.**

## Writing the outline

Now you are finally ready to set your ideas out on paper. An outline provides a skeleton on which to hang your ideas. An outline is an exercise in judgement. You are deciding what value each idea or fact has and how it relates to the other ideas and facts and to your main point.

Outlining operates by a process of division. You divide the ideas and facts into at least two segments. Then you divide them again, and again. As you divide them you begin to see more clearly the relationship between the different parts of your idea.

It is then much easier to work out how they relate to each other. As you divide you also begin to set up further categories into which each of them fits. This ability to set up categories and assign things to them is one of the specialised activities of the human brain, which is more efficient and quicker at classifying information than your computer.

By setting your ideas out in a clear logical order, classified into categories that make sense to you, you make clear to yourself and to your reader the way in which you see the subject. If you can logically order the ideas and facts you want to present, the reader too will grasp that order when reading the document. So not only does preparing an outline force you to see the shape and set up a logical ordering of your ideas, it also conveys that order to the reader. Conversely a haphazard order will reveal a lack of order in your reasoning.

In addition, try to order your subject in a way that will be meaningful to your readers. Think about the way they view the subject. It may be necessary to expand one section and go into it in greater depth because it is not familiar to them even though you know it backwards and forwards.

In your office report you know quite well how much training those new employees require but how much do the members of the Board of Directors, your primary audience, know about the employees? Not much, probably. Expand the section on the need for training.

**Don't lose sight of your audience or of your purpose.**

## Guide to your outline

1   Always start your outline with a statement of your main point. Then write one sentence summarising your introduction.

2   Divide the subject into major headings. Try not to use more than five because the outline then becomes unwieldy. If you do have more than five go back to step four and start rethinking your subject and re-analysing your data.

3   Dividing your subject will force you to list your ideas and facts in a hierarchy of importance in support of your main point. Some ideas, or facts, will be discarded during the process. Others will need further development because you will find that you do not have enough to convince your reader.

   **The more you can develop your thoughts at this point and set out your specific facts, the less you will have to think about them when you are faced with writing your draft.**

4   List the most important ideas with lots of white space left between these major points. This first level of division of ideas will be assigned Roman numerals (I, II, III, IV). (See page 40 for a sample outline.)

5   Then further divide each level of the Roman numerals, working through one at a time. So, divide I into at least two parts. After that move on to divide level II, and so on to III, IV and V, through all of the Roman numerals you need.

   Label this second level with capital letters (A, B, C, D).

6   After going through each of the Roman numerals and further dividing them, go back and look at the capital letters to see if any of them

should be further divided. Label this next level of the outline with Arabic numerals (1, 2, 3, 4). If you divide any of these levels again you can use small letters (*a, b, c, d*).

You do not have to divide each new level. You can leave some undivided. You can divide just a level 2, but not necessarily the 1 that preceded it. It probably is not useful to divide any level further than *(a), (b)* and *(c)*. The example on page 40 demonstrates how this looks.

Once you feel comfortable with the outline form you can adapt it to your own uses. We are presenting this format to explain the method of outlining. Later you may decide to use a different system.

Some people use decimals of Arabic numerals, such as 1, 1.1, 1.2, 1.2.1 and so on. This can be quite confusing at the outline stage although it may be useful in the final document. (See the **Benslow Report** on pages 114–137.) Using the combination of numerals and letters makes the different levels of the outline jump out at you so it is easier to see the distinctions being made. But what do you think? Try it both ways and see which you are more comfortable with. Think up a system that you feel good about. Whatever system you adopt what matters is that it is clear to the reader. If you are doing an outline which your supervisor will see, make sure you discuss the method with the supervisor. On the next page is an example of one possible outline for the situation we have been talking about.

### Outline for Report on the
### Functioning of the Office

23 April 19___

MAIN POINT: In order to compete successfully in our product market over the next five years at least half of the 40 staff members in Section D of our Department must receive advanced technical training sometime this year.

INTRODUCTION: Although Section D contains 20 experienced, fully trained staff, the additional 20 members hired in the past two years lack important technical expertise and training in our latest products.

I.  One quarter of the present staff have been hired in the past six months.
    A. They were all hired for their high level of intelligence and general knowledge of our field.
    B. We selected these particular people with the knowledge that within a year we would have to provide them with technical training.
    C. Since that year is up we will now begin to lose productivity if they are not trained.
II. One quarter of the new staff hired over a year ago never received any training at all.
III. The Training Society offers a three-part training course that fits their needs perfectly.
    A. The course is designed around the technical aspects of our product.
       1. It covers the most complicated aspects of our technical procedure.
       2. The course leader is an experienced professional in the field.
    B. Six of our staff received this training last year.
       1. Results of the training showed up immediately in increased production from each of the six.
       2. The benefits of the training remained with them, according to the study I conducted on their productivity and skill after 12 months. (Study attached in Appendix A.)

CONCLUSION: It makes sense to send the 20 new staff members on The Training Society's course as soon as possible.

Having finished your outline go back over it to make sure you have covered all important topics and that you have the material to back up each. Fill in additional levels with the details which you will use in your document to prove your point. The more thoroughly you can fill in each section now, the less work you will have at the writing stage.

## Checklist

Use this checklist to make sure you have a successful and accurate outline.

1 Ensure that what you had expressed as the main point really is your main point, now that you have written out all the ideas. If the emphasis has changed, restate your main point.

2 See that the Introduction contains the appropriate material to introduce the reader to the subject.

3 Now that you have laid out the main points ask yourself whether they still make sense to you and seem logical. A sub-point, for instance, may now seem worthy of being a main point. Rearrange the outline to accommodate any changes you feel are needed.

4 Make sure you have no more than five major points. If you have more, rethink the outline. Maybe you are trying to cover too much. Maybe the order or subdivisions are not correct.

5 Make sure the subdivisions are accurate and logical.

6 Make sure that all points on a single level are equal in importance. The $A$ should equal the $B$ and the $C$ in logical importance.

# Writing patterns

Professional writers use various techniques, or patterns, to help them organise their material. They do this with little conscious thought as they gain in experience. If they were taught to write in school then probably someone pointed out these patterns to them, helping them to edit and rewrite until their prose became smoother, clearer, simpler. Often writers assimilate these patterns through experience in thinking and reading but are not aware that they know them. Before we proceed further it will be useful to review these patterns.

## *Example*

Probably the most frequently used pattern of exposition is example. We all use examples in everyday speech and so it should be easy to transfer that use to our professional work.

When you cite an example you attempt to get the reader to understand what you are talking about by presenting a sample or instance of the idea you are discussing. You are probably aware from using this book that we have been looking at examples throughout.

Some writers hesitate to give concrete examples, thinking that the reader will not care to hear about trivial things. This is a misconception because good examples are not trivial; they are a necessary device to make your writing clear to your reader. Readers are grateful for all the help you can provide.

## *Analogy*

Similar to the example is the analogy, a device for clarifying your material by comparing or relating it to something else your reader already knows. This takes a double act of imagination: first you must stretch your mind to find a thing, person or situation comparable to what you are talking about; second you must put yourself in the reader's place to determine whether your reader will understand your analogy. It is no good citing an analogy which the reader has never heard of or cannot imagine.

If, for instance, you were explaining that the atmosphere in your office was analogous to the atmosphere in Winston Churchill's war cabinet, the clever insight you are making would be lost if your readers had no idea what Churchill's war cabinet was like, let alone who Winston Churchill was.

You should restrict analogy to those occasions when you know your audience well. If you know your document is liable to be read by an unknown audience then analogy is not appropriate. Nor is it appropriate if there is a chance the analogy may become outdated.

Be sure that your analogy actually works; that is, be sure that the two things being compared are in fact comparable. The following analogy fails because a computer disc does not function in the same way as a car engine:

> *A computer without a disc is like a car without an engine.*

## Classification

Classification is a process of sorting items into categories. Setting up categories for filing is perhaps the most common example of classification.

Here are three strategies for more effective classifying.

1   Every item under consideration must be able to fit into one of the categories you have set up. If you are left with one or more items for which no category seems suitable something is wrong with your classification method. Add another category or two, or go back and completely rework your categories.

2   No category should overlap another category. If you were listing areas under which insurance claims could be made, it would not be helpful to have one category called *Fire* and another called *Arson* since fire and arson overlap. Change the categories to something like *Accidental fire* and *Arson*.

3   Each category should be clearly named. Another insurance claim category called *Theft* might not be clear. Does it include both in-house pilfering and break-ins? Then use these names instead of *Theft*.

Classification is not a difficult pattern to use. You can use it in helping to set up your outline. Each category that you decide on can become a section of the outline. If you can establish your categories at the start of your thinking about a piece of writing you can sort your data as they come to you.

You can also use classification to help explain any complex subject by dividing it into categories.

## Definition

A definition tells your readers what something is. You can define an object, a procedure, a term or a concept. Use the definition to give your readers a precise idea of your subject. If there is even the slightest chance that your readers do not have a clear idea of your subject, define it. If there is a chance that they have a different idea from yours, define the idea as you are using it. Clear definitions are especially important when writing about something new.

**Get into the habit of clearly defining any terms that might possibly cause confusion.**

There are three basic kinds of definition.

**The short definition** explains an object or idea with a synonym or short phrase. It is often set off between commas or in brackets after the word or phrase being defined. Its aim is to offer the reader a quick definition without halting the flow of the sentence. Consider the following short definitions in italics:

> Construction workers in Arctic regions must take into account the presence of hummocks, which are *rounded knolls* (or *ridges*), *sometimes composed of ice.*

(Notice that '*or ridges*' serves as a short definition within a short definition.)

**The sentence definition** is a little more comprehensive than the short definition primarily because it follows a specific format. The sentence definition is made up of two sections, the class and those things that distinguish it from all other items in the same class.

A pen, we might say, belongs to the class of *writing instruments*, though we could also narrow it to *hand-held writing instruments*. What distinguishes the particular item from all others in the class is that a pen *uses ink*. Thus a pen is a *hand-held writing instrument that uses ink*.

Examples of sentence definition can be found in the **glossary** at the end of many reports or books. They also provide useful introductory sentences when discussing a new concept or object.

**An extended definition** can be as short as a paragraph or as long as a chapter. An extended definition may include a brief history of the term (what language it came from, how it entered professional use, how its meaning has changed). It should also state its function, both in its immediate use and in a wider, more general context.

---

An extended definition will make use of many of the other patterns of writing discussed in this section. It is useful to provide examples in support of your extended definition. It is also sometimes effective to use contrast to define something by showing what it is not. Concern for children in a nursery school, for instance, is *not just seeing that they play safely*; it is also encouraging them to engage in various constructive activities.

---

Here is a sequence of steps to help you write an extended definition.

1   Establish the point of view from which you will be writing your definition. Are you, for instance, defining a compact disc player from the point of view of a user or from the point of view of an electronics expert?

2   Determine the class to which the term or object belongs.

3   Set out those characteristics of your object or concept that make it different from all the others with which it might be confused.

4   Choose a pattern to define it, such as classification or comparison/ contrast.

5   Think of other examples which are similar to it, but not the same.

6   Eliminate all the things that are like it but are not it. This process of eliminating everything else narrows the focus to just your term.

7   Identify any specific details particular to the item, without which it
would not be itself.

8   Make sure that no other term can be defined by your criteria.

9   Double check that your term stands for what you have written and for
nothing else.

**Exercise**

1   Write a definition for a cross-head screwdriver which enables
your reader to distinguish it from all other screwdrivers.
Establish first the class to which it belongs. It will be
necessary to look at and perhaps draw comparisons with
other types of screwdriver in order to set out the ways it
differs from other items in the class while remaining within
that class. For example, the colour of the handle of a
screwdriver does not affect its classification at all.

2   Take a coin out of your pocket or purse and define it.

3   Define your job.

## Cause and effect

Cause and effect analyses why something happened. Cause and effect is a
useful pattern but it must be used carefully and correctly; otherwise your
entire discussion may collapse.

The difficulty in thinking out this pattern is in determining which is cause
and which is effect. Often something that is quickly labelled *cause* is only
another *effect*; the real or true cause is harder to determine. To arrive at
the underlying or ultimate causes of something examine the situation
from every angle. Search for the cause furthest back, the true cause.
This requires persistence, imagination and courage – courage because
what you discover to be the true cause may not be flattering or profitable.

In British Rail's notorious excuse a few years ago for the failure of their
new trains to run during a snowstorm, the cause was given as 'the wrong
kind of snow'. The public scorn that followed stemmed from the view that
faulty design, not the kind of snow, was the true cause.

Several pitfalls lie in wait for the writer who tries too quickly or superficially to determine cause. It is important to keep several things in mind when attempting cause and effect.

- Be open-minded. Do not be quick to decide on the ultimate cause of something.
- Be as logical about your search for cause as you can. This is not the time to let your own preferences or prejudices determine your findings.
- Never assume that juxtaposition of either time or place is the result of cause. Eliminate coincidence.
- Make sure you are taking all factors into account. Are there more effects than were at first apparent? Are there actually more causes than appeared at first?
- Trace every link between the elements you are examining to make sure that you do not miss any.
- Make sure you have traced the elements back as far as you can to determine the ultimate cause.
- Know whether you are searching for immediate causes, underlying causes or ultimate causes.

## Example

**A lorry driver crashed his lorry.**

| | |
|---|---|
| *Immediate cause* | He fell asleep. |
| *Underlying cause* | He was working long hours. |
| *Ultimate cause* | Irresponsible managers ignored laws on scheduling. |

Again, as always, check the **audience** and the **purpose** of what you are doing. What may be a cause from one point of view is clearly not the cause from another. A police report might indicate that the man holding the smoking gun caused the victim's death. The coroner's report might indicate that a bullet entering the heart caused the victim's death. A psychiatrist's report might indicate that a sense of sexual inadequacy caused the man to take out his frustrations by shooting the victim. And so on and on.

## *Comparison and contrast*

In comparison and contrast you are examining items or factors for their similarities or for their differences. When you look at similarities you are comparing. When you look at differences you are contrasting. You can use them separately but often you combine the two. In that case you show the common features first and then the differences.

Traders offer comparisons and contrasts all the time when trying to persuade a customer or client to purchase something from them rather than from someone else. They show first how their product is like other products, then how it is different (superior, of course!).

The elements compared or contrasted must relate to each other. It must make sense to draw the comparison. You would not, for example, compare the advantages of hauling freight by rail in Great Britain with shipping it across the Atlantic in a container ship.

Comparison/contrast also offers a way of setting up items or ideas against each other. Year-end personnel appraisals offer a comparison or contrast of one employee's skills and performance against a standard set up by the company.

Here are some steps you can follow in planning comparison/contrast.

1   Before you can set up your comparison and contrast you need to establish the criteria or standards by which you will judge the items. It is impossible to judge, for instance, whether your company should move to an industrial estate or remain in the town centre without first establishing criteria by which to judge between the industrial estate and the town centre. Think of as many criteria as you can: cost (of the move, of new stationery, or rent and rates), convenience (for the company's employees, for clients or customers, for deliveries), prestige, size of premises, neighbouring businesses, security, safety and so on. Now you have a means for judging between the two.

2   After establishing your criteria, put them in order of importance. This order may be hard to determine, even controversial, but until you know your priorities you may be able to compare and contrast but you cannot draw any conclusions. The town centre may score higher than the industrial estate on most of the criteria, but if safety is one of

your priorities and the town centre is less safe than the industrial estate, you will probably choose the industrial estate.

3   Once you have established your criteria and set them out in order of importance, you must decide whether to organise your paragraphs vertically or horizontally. You can either go through all criteria in item A and then all in item B (vertical), or show how item A and item B measure up against the first criterion, then how against the second, and so on (horizontal).

In other words, you can either first evaluate the town centre on cost, convenience, prestige, etc. and then evaluate the industrial estate by the same criteria (being sure you don't switch the order of the criteria when you list them). Or you can focus on cost and compare the town centre to the industrial estate, then move on to the convenience of the town centre as opposed to the industrial estate and so on. (See the examples below and on page 50.)

Which method of organising you choose will depend on your purpose and the occasion. The basic rule here is that your reader should be able to remember item A while reading about item B.

Sometimes in a presentation with two flipcharts you can run through all of item A and then, switching to the other chart, list all the factors for item B. That way the people in the audience can compare them by shifting their eyes from one chart to the other. Which method you choose may also depend on how complicated your subject is or which factor you want your audience to linger over or to remember.

---

**Vertical comparison/contrast**

|   | I. Town Centre |   | II. Industrial Estate |
|---|---|---|---|
| A. | Cost | A. | Cost |
| B. | Convenience | B. | Convenience |
| C. | Prestige | C. | Prestige |
| D. | Size of premises | D. | Size of premises |
| E. | Neighbourhood | E. | Neighbourhood |
| F. | Security | F. | Security |
| G. | Safety | G. | Safety |

---

If you are comparing and contrasting three, four or more items, it is useful to accompany your text with a table. This table can then be read either horizontally or vertically, depending on whether one reads across or down.

The two sample outlines on page 49 and below show the structure of vertical and horizontal comparison/contrasts.

| **Horizontal comparison/contrast** | | | |
|---|---|---|---|
| I. | Cost | V. | Neighbourhood |
| | A.  Town Centre | | A.  Town Centre |
| | B.  Industrial Estate | | B.  Industrial Estate |
| II. | Convenience | VI. | Security |
| | A.  Town Centre | | A.  Town Centre |
| | B.  Industrial Estate | | B.  Industrial Estate |
| III. | Prestige | VII. | Safety |
| | A.  Town Centre | | A.  Town Centre |
| | B.  Industrial Estate | | B.  Industrial Estate |
| IV. | Size of premises | | |
| | A.  Town Centre | | |
| | B.  Industrial Estate | | |

## *Process analysis*

The analysis of a process is, at its simplest, merely the listing of steps taken when carrying out a set of actions, such as getting dressed in the morning. Process analysis is at the heart of each set of instructions which you may read or have to write. It can be used in a number of other ways in a proposal (to explain how a procedure will work) or in a technical report (to make sure your readers understand what you are talking about before you begin discussing an operation).

A process analysis is an explanation of how something works. At the core of any set of instructions, or user manual for a new electronics system, a computer program or a laboratory experiment, lies an analysis of a process taking place. In each of these activities you proceed step by step, and your writing about them must also proceed step by step. The steps must occur in a particular order. If they do not, the process will not work. Each step must be included in your analysis.

Process analysis can be used in many different kinds of reports and memorandums. Basically, though, it is used to accomplish one of two things: it either *informs* the audience how something is done, or can be done, or has been done, and thus merely provides information; or it can be used to *instruct*, to tell someone exactly how to do something. Make sure you know which you are doing before you start writing.

Surgeons in the operating theatre, for example, write up notes explaining exactly what they did and how they performed the operation to *inform* other doctors about how it was done or could be done. But when they are lecturing to young medical students on how to perform the operation they would be more precise, giving *instructions*, not only in greater detail but in shorter sentences. If you are merely informing someone it would not be a disaster if you provided the process in a slightly less detailed way. In the operating theatre that slight difference could cost someone's life.

Process is also used to analyse a situation, especially one that is highly complex. It reduces the situation to something that is easily grasped, such as a complicated political chain of command.

Process analysis is often used in argument, either to build it up or reduce it to rubbish. It is often used in courtrooms or boardrooms with some-what less detail to point out flaws in an opponent's argument. It can also form part of a complicated comparison and contrast as a way to build up the comparison further.

The most frequent use of process analysis is to explain, rather than to instruct. Perhaps you can begin to see that a familiarity with process analysis can benefit your writing and your ability to lay out an issue, to argue a point. Use it often. Become used to it. Start with the simple exercise here and then consciously begin to use it in other situations. It will make an enormous difference to the clarity of your writing about complicated issues.

Process analysis is the most difficult of the various patterns. Many documents are weak because they lack the analysis of a critical process or because the writer began a process analysis and veered off into narrative or instructions.

A formal process analysis has four distinct parts. It doesn't matter what you label them in your document or manual or report but you should include all four parts:

1 introduction;
2 list of each step of the process;
3 explanation of each step;
4 conclusion.

## 1 Introduction

Introduce your readers to the need for a process analysis and the function it serves in your broader topic. The introduction may include a definition of the term you are writing about, a description of the equipment or material, a history of the subject, your particular focus and purpose (why you are writing a process analysis). It may list the equipment needed, as, for instance, at the beginning of a recipe. Keep the introduction as short and precise as you can.

## 2 List of steps

This section is simply a numbered list, running vertically down the page (as in the list above) with enough white space to make it easy to read. The list of steps must be in the correct order and must include each step. Write the list in simple sentences. Do not go into detail at this point.

## 3 Explanation of each step

The explanation is the crucial section (the body) since it discusses just how each step works and how you get from one step to the next. Write each explanation in a separate paragraph so you have as many paragraphs as you have steps, making the transition from one paragraph to the next the actual transition from one step to the next. This requires a lot of thought about the function of each step, but with a little practice it will become easy.

## 4 Conclusion

You conclude by relating everything you have written so far to the whole subject you are writing about. It may fit into a future project or procedure. Tie everything together in this final paragraph, which can be quite short. You can also use it to lead the reader on to another process analysis.

If you find yourself writing up more than ten or twelve steps you are probably trying to write up more than one process. Go back and rethink.

It is sometimes a good idea when faced with a long list of steps to divide it into three, four, or five major steps each containing several minor steps. Perhaps you could combine several steps into one major step and several subordinate steps.

It might turn out, however, that you discover you should be writing two (or more) processes instead of one. Each process should be analysing and listing only the most important steps. If someone has to complete another process before proceeding with yours, that needs to be made very clear at the beginning.

## Exercise 1

All of us go through a series of steps each morning when we get up. List the steps you take each morning (excluding Sunday and holidays) to get out of bed, dress and get out of the house. Begin with the ringing of the alarm clock (or whatever you use to wake up). List each step (but do not list each separate little step such as brushing each tooth). List them in the order in which you do them. Make sure you include all the steps. One man listed all his but when he read it over to a friend he realised he had left the house without putting his trousers on! Another man put shoes on but forgot his socks.

## Exercise 2

Choose a relatively simple procedure at work which you are very familiar with and try to write down the steps necessary to complete it. Do not list more than 12 steps. List them in the correct order. Use simple clear short sentences. Do not attempt in your list to explain how to do any of them. This is just a practice list.

Remember process analysis on its own is not the same as instructions. A process analysis is concerned with *stating what happens when some kind of change is taking place*; a set of instructions *gives commands telling people how to carry out the process.* Instructions are organised like process analyses, but they are aimed at different readers. (See pages 145–50 for further discussion of **instructions**.)

## Questions to ask yourself

Ask yourself these questions to check that you are considering all the options.

**Narration**
(i)     Have you been asked to tell a story?
(ii)    Is the chronological account of the event necessary for your audience's understanding?
(iii)   Are there legal requirements for the recounting of the precise chronology of the event?
(iv)    If you are filling in a form is there a space that requires you to give a narrative account?
(v)     Have you included all the pertinent persons, places, times and descriptions?
(vi)    Have you excluded information that is unnecessary?

**Description**
(i)     Is a description of the object or person or place essential to your purpose?
(ii)    Have you included precise and accurate measurements and characteristics?
(iii)   Have you written the description in terminology your audience can understand?
(iv)    Have you maintained the same position throughout?
(v)     Have you included any illustrations that could help your reader see more clearly?

**Argument**
(i)     Have you been asked to argue?
(ii)    Have you considered all sides of the issue?
(iii)   Is your argument logical?

## Exposition

If you are using **examples**:

(i)     have you included enough examples?

(ii)    do your examples provide enough concrete detail?

If you are using **classification**:

(i)     is there a category for every item you are classifying?

(ii)    should you add another category to your classification system?

(iii)   do any of your categories overlap?

(iv)    are all the categories of equal importance?

(v)     do the names of the categories clearly describe the items contained in the categories?

If you are using **comparison/contrast**:

(i)     are the objects you are comparing similar enough to make a comparison valid?

(ii)    are the objects you are contrasting dissimilar enough to make a contrast valid?

(iii)   is horizontal or vertical contrast more effective?

(iv)    have you provided a conclusion that pulls the items together?

If you are using **cause and effect**:

(i)     have you investigated the situation from every angle to discover all the effects?

(ii)    have you searched as far as possible for the true causes?

(iii)   are you sure you haven't confused cause with what was only an effect?

If you are using **definition**:

(i)     are you sure your definition applies to your term and to no other?

(ii)    in a short definition is the word used actually a synonym?

(iii)   in a sentence definition have you placed the item in the most accurate class?

(iv)    have you distinguished this item from all others in its class?

(v)     in an extended definition do you need to include the history of the term, examples of its usage, differences in usage?

(vi)    have you considered any other of the patterns of exposition to help define your term?

If you are using **process analysis**:

(i)     have you listed each step of the process?

(ii)    are you sure you haven't forgotten any steps that you might have taken for granted?

(iii)    are the steps in the correct order?

(iv)    have you listed all the equipment or material needed to complete the process?

(v)    have you fully explained each step?

(vi)    have you told the reader how you get from one step to the next?

(vii)    have you written a conclusion tying it all together?

# Style

## Definition

There can be many different definitions of style, but when we use the word in this book we are referring to the type of language a writer uses. Writers often express an individual style in their writing, though this is more common in creative writing than business writing. In business writing individuals are less important than the subject they are writing about. The style used should draw attention to the subject, rather than to the individual writer.

Some people think that the way to make a document interesting is to write in an elaborate or unusual style. Instead of saying, *Next week we shall publish this year's Annual Report,* these people might be tempted to say *Seven days from now we shall lay before the public our latest Annual Report.* Perhaps such fancy writing may be appropriate for some kinds of advertising (often tongue in cheek), but seldom for other kinds of business writing. This style does not make a document interesting; it makes it funny, and the joke is at the expense of the writer. It is rather like turning up to a business meeting in fancy dress: who can take what you say seriously?

**Remember: your aim is to draw attention to what you are saying, not to how you are saying it. Don't let your writing style get in the way of your subject.**

## Different levels of style

When we talk of style we usually divide it into three levels: formal, informal and colloquial. These three divisions do not have rigid boundaries: for example, the minutes of board meetings for a family company may be written in a style that falls somewhere between the formal and the informal. A letter written in an informal style may draw upon a few colloquial expressions to produce a particular effect.

Regardless of which style you are using, you are still expected to write in standard, grammatically correct English, which means writing in complete sentences with correct spelling and appropriate punctuation.

## Formal style

The formal style is impersonal, like the stereotyped butler, who is simply there, doing his job efficiently. The aim of this impersonality is to raise the document beyond merely local and individual concerns. Idiosyncratic language and jargon (see pages 97–8) do not belong in the formal style. A proposal to supply a local council with plastic dustbins, for instance, will be credible only in so far as it is written in the formal language the council usually uses. This language might use long words (coming from Latin and Greek), which the writer would never use in conversation. This language can sound rather stilted and legalistic.

---

For many people a document not in a formal style sounds unprofessional and therefore lacking in validity. If you are writing for these people then be sure to use a formal style.

---

### Absence of personal pronouns

The most conspicuous feature of formal writing is the absence of personal pronouns. On pages 29–31 we looked at the way personal pronouns can lighten the tone of a document. Here we are looking at the way eliminating them can formalise the style. It does this by effacing the people involved and therefore increasing the objectivity.

The supplier of plastic dustbins could say in the proposal,

> *Our calculations show that you will have to replace an estimated 300 dustbins a year because of vandalism.*

The formal style would avoid 'our' (since it should not be just *our* calculations that show this but *any* calculations) and 'you' (since the supplier is speaking to the council in its official capacity). Thus the formal version would be:

*Calculations show that the council will need to replace an estimated 300 dustbins a year.*

The passive voice is another way to eliminate personal pronouns. (See pages 92–3.) You must be careful, however, that your use of the passive does not make your sentences vague in any way. The sentence about replacing dustbins could be rewritten using passives:

*It is calculated that an estimated 300 dustbins will need to be replaced each year.*

The danger is that this sentence removes all reference to the council and to any agent responsible for the calculations. Perhaps it is evident from the context that the council will be replacing the dustbins; if not, then notice the potential confusion over whether the council or the supplier will be responsible for replacing the dustbins. You could get around this problem by adding that the dustbins will need to be replaced *by the council*, but by this point your sentence has become too indirect and the responsibility too diffused. You would be better off forgetting about the passive.

Another reason for eliminating personal pronouns in the formal style is to avoid ambiguity or confusion. Suppose the dustbin supplier said,

*We will need to calculate the number of residents in each road.*

Who is this *we*? Is it the supplier, or the supplier and the council who together will make the calculation? You can see how this could easily become a legal problem.

Or suppose the supplier said,

*It will be your responsibility to see that the dustbins are cleaned once a year.*

By saying *your responsibility*, the writer seems to be addressing only the people in the sanitation department, but there may be other readers. Most reports have a variety of readers (see pages 12–15) and there is a good chance that the proposal will be read not only by someone in the sanitation department but also by someone in the council's contracting office, who will *not* be responsible for cleaning the bins. To use 'your' in this case gives the impression that you were unprofessional and forgot about your secondary audience.

### Aiming for conciseness

Another feature of the formal style is conciseness. All writing should avoid unnecessary words and ideas, but formal writing should be particularly economical. In the past the formal style was equated with an elaborate, expansive use of language, which we today find unnecessary and obstructive. When you are writing in the formal style, be sure to be direct and to avoid wordiness. (See page 99.)

## *Informal style*

The informal style is more relaxed than the formal style. But this does not mean it is an excuse for sloppy writing, just as informal dress does not mean torn jeans and offensive T-shirts. Like the formal style, the informal style uses complete sentences and correct grammar, and avoids slang. Informal writing often makes use of personal pronouns and contractions to relax the sentences. It can include everyday words so long as they are not confusing or vague, and it avoids technical words whenever possible.

The informal style invites a more personal, subjective approach to the material. At its best, it is refreshing and emphasises the truth that communication passes from person to person, not from machine to machine.

It is hard to make rigid rules about what kinds of writing ask for an informal, as opposed to a formal, style. One suggestion is to consider the relationship between the writer and the reader. If their jobs are on the same level, or if they know each other and have been communicating together for some time, they may use a more informal style. Communication passing from lower-ranking staff to higher-ranking or vice versa tends to use a more formal style. If the document is passing between organisations, the relationship between the organisations is important. Again, if the two companies are of equal status or if the companies are friendly towards each other, the writers may use a less formal informal style.

**If you are in the slightest doubt whether to use a formal or informal style use the more formal style or ask your manager. Even though you know the person, your letter forms a legal record in both companies. In other words, any business communication is never entirely informal, never just a communication between two people. It is a communication between two organisations.**

### Exercise

Take a letter or memorandum you wrote recently and rewrite it in a less formal style. Then rewrite it in a more formal style.

## Colloquial style

The colloquial style is the kind of language we speak but do not usually write unless we are writing a personal letter or dialogue in fiction. This style is characterised by the use of slang. It is colourful but too casual for all but the most unusual business occasions.

Not only is slang too casual; it is also dangerous since slang is rarely precise. Slang expressions are unstable: their meanings change sometimes month by month; people in different regions or of different ages or from different backgrounds may mean different things by the same slang words.

The colloquial style also tends to throw into sentences what are called interrupters – little words and expressions that serve to waste time while we think what to say next. It should be obvious that such expressions as *well, really* and *you know* (e.g. *Well, I really need those items now, you know*) have no place in business writing.

## Other styles

Besides the three levels of style – formal, informal and colloquial – we need to recognise a few other styles.

## Old-fashioned style

An old-fashioned style is characterised by archaic words such as *albeit* or *howsoever* and by certain flourishes, most notably at the close of letters (e.g. *I remain your most obedient . . .*). Not many people deliberately use this style, but watch out that you don't fall into it unawares.

Another characteristic that can date your writing is using masculine pronouns when referring to men and women. A sentence such as,

> *Each member of the committee should receive his copies of the minutes*

will feel outdated to those readers who are aware that today we try to avoid expressions that exclude 50 per cent of the human race. Many people would prefer to see something like,

> *All members of the committee should receive their copies of the minutes.*

## American style

The American style in business writing can often be more informal than the British style, yet at times it can also be much more cumbersome and bureaucratic. If it happens that you have to produce a document in an American style, it would be a good idea to study other American documents in the same field to get a sense of how the style may differ from the one you are used to. It might be a good idea to ask an American to read it, or even call in an American consultant if it is important to get the style right. It is also useful to know the differences between American and British spelling and usage. There are several reference books which can help such as *The British/American Dictionary* by Norman Moss (Arrow Books, 1990).

## Private language

Private language is the language one group of workers or one particular company may develop to speak in-house about its work. It often takes the form of abbreviations, acronyms or nicknames. Private language provides a handy short cut, but if you use it you must be sure that all of your readers know what you are talking about or are provided with a key (e.g. a glossary). Avoid private language for any writing that may be going out-of-house. Avoid it too for documents that you know will be filed and may be needed for future use; who is to say that what passes for private language today will still be intelligible in a few years' time when the document may be read again?

Here is an example of private language, unintelligible to anyone not working in the same area as the writer:

*Interpretation of the signal created by the PSP is done by the CDU and sent to the system computer.*

## House style

Most large organisations have a house style. Besides telling you whether to use contractions or how to lay out a page, it will guide you with little quirks such as how junior colleagues address senior colleagues or vice versa. There is an unwritten code in the Civil Service, for instance, that all civil servants when writing to other civil servants sign the letter *yours ever.*

---

### A note about E-Mail

It is so easy to send messages through computer systems like E-mail that some people get carried away and add personal messages at the end of their business message. Some couch a business message in private language or even (since the rapid flow of messages back and forth can seem like a real conversation) in colloquial style. These people should remember that their messages might need to be passed on to a secondary reader or be filed away. It is a good idea therefore to avoid a style that might embarrass the sender or the receiver or show them in an unprofessional light. Has the writer of the FAX on page 156 gone too far or not?

---

# 2

## THE ROUGH DRAFT

If you are writing a simple or routine memorandum or letter and you have
a clear idea of what you want to say, you might be able to write the piece
straight off from your outline. If, however, you have to write something
new or complex you will probably need to adjust your writing to make
sure it is saying exactly what you want it to say and in the right order. To
do this you will need one or more drafts where you can experiment with
different approaches and styles.

Rough drafts are also important in those situations when your writing
needs approval from your supervisor or from another department. The
draft represents a tentative version of the document that you can expect
to change after seeing comments and suggestions from other people.

### *Turning your outline into sentences*

You should eventually work out your own way of developing a rough
draft, but here are some helpful guidelines. Your aim is simply to produce
a basic draft that you will later amplify, revise and correct. If you are
working on an unfamiliar or complex piece of writing you will already have
drawn up an outline. (See pages 31–41.) The outline makes your job
much easier since you need not worry about what you are going to say

next. All you need to concentrate on is turning the notes in the outline into sentences. If you are not working from an outline simply start writing and carry on until you have covered all the material you need to cover.

Some people take their rough draft too seriously and think it should be as well written as possible. This is a misconception. No one expects the rough draft to be free from errors; it exists to be changed and improved.

---

Here are four cautions to heed when writing your rough draft.

● Do not stop to read over what you have written until you finish the draft: work as fast as you can.
● Do not worry about your writing style or about correctness: this draft is for your eyes only.
● Do not run to a dictionary to check spelling: no one cares at this stage, and anyway the word you want to look up may be deleted by the time you get to your final draft.
● Do not go back to check on your data or re-evaluate your findings: make a note to do that later.

---

## Overcoming writer's block

Like any writer you are bound to find at some time or other that you simply cannot start writing. You may even begin to panic as your deadline gets nearer and nearer and you still have not turned out a draft. The following stratagems that experienced writers use to overcome writer's block may help you.

### Approach the writing with a relaxed and confident attitude

If you are relaxed and confident, you have a greater chance of overcoming your panic. The quickest way to relax is to breathe deeply. Before you begin to write, sit back and breathe deeply and slowly three times. This will relax your nerves and at the same time prepare your mind for concentrating. If you find yourself particularly tense when starting to write, it might be worth looking into a book teaching relaxation techniques.

If you know what you are writing about, you should have no trouble feeling confident. Build on your confidence. Remind yourself that you know what there is to say; you know who your reader is. Now just relax and tell the reader what you have to say. (Of course if you don't know what you are writing about, should you even be attempting a draft yet? Go back and find out what you should be saying.)

## If you feel daunted when facing a blank page, work gradually by enlarging your outline

If you feel panicked by the thought of starting off a rough draft from scratch, go back to your outline and expand one section of it. Keep adding to it word by word. Rewrite the phrases or sentences to produce a short paragraph. Go on to the next section and do the same. By the time you have gone through the whole outline, you will have produced a first draft without noticing it.

An alternative to this method is to write up two or three pages of whatever comes to your mind about a particular section just to start the flow of words.

## Start writing in the middle

Choose the material you feel most comfortable with and write up that part first. Then go on to another section you feel comfortable with an write up that one. After writing two or three easy sections, you should build up momentum that will enable you to tackle the harder sections with less trouble.

## Try to eliminate distractions

Examine the place where you write and determine which distractions you can live with and which you need to do something about. If the telephone keeps ringing or people keep coming in with questions or requests, see whether you can disconnect the telephone, hide yourself away in another room or find another time to write when there will be fewer physical distractions.

Remember to control internal distractions too. Concentration is such hard work that most of us are ready to seize on anything that will distract our minds from the writing. Few people ever achieve perfect concentration, but if you become aware of the distractions you generate yourself, you can work at reducing their number and their frequency.

### Discover which medium works best for you

If your writing is blocked, try moving from the keyboard to pen and paper, and from pen and paper to the keyboard. Since most of us find it easier to talk about a subject than to write about it, you may even want to try speaking your draft into a tape recorder or dictating it to a secretary. Experiment with which medium feels most comfortable to you.

### If you do not seem able to make any progress, return to pre-writing and clarify your ideas

Sometimes writers cannot make their sentences flow because their ideas are not clear. If after several attempts you find yourself deleting more sentences than you are keeping, go back to the pre-writing stage and rethink and replan.

**Be suspicious if you are reluctant to write. It may be your mind telling you that you have not finished thinking about your ideas.**

## *Guidelines to effective dictation*

Many people find the idea of dictating a draft very daunting. The prospect of having to think out loud can seem threatening. Yet if you speak to those people who regularly use dictation, they will tell you that in a short while they got used to this new medium and now would not be without it. So it is worth giving dictation a try.

When dictating, it is more essential than ever to have some sort of outline in front of you. Do not trust yourself to dictate off the top of your head unless you are dictating a short, routine letter. Even a brief outline of three or four key words on a slip of paper will suffice to direct you once you start speaking.

One advantage of dictating your draft instead of writing is that it does not involve as much physical work. You are not wielding a pen or tapping keys but simply sitting and talking. There is thus a smaller barrier between you and your words and you can usually produce more words more quickly.

But be aware that dictation tends to produce more material. Be prepared to edit your draft thoroughly to make it concise.

Another, even more important advantage of dictation is that because you are speaking you are less likely to produce long, pompous sentences that no one can read. But do not become so relaxed in your dictation that you slip into a colloquial style. (See page 60.)

The chief disadvantage of dictating is that it is hard to review what you have just produced. If you are writing your draft you can always leaf through the pages to see the document as a whole, but when you listen to a tape you have produced by dictation you cannot easily examine what came before. You lose the relationship of what you are hearing to the document as a whole. You have to wait until your typist produces a hard copy before you can do much substantial editing.

When dictating, you have the added job of thinking not only of your reader but also of the person listening to the dictation. Follow these rules of courtesy.

1   Speak clearly. Be aware of words that may sound confusing (e.g. *presence* and *presents*) and spell them out.

2   Speak slowly. A typist listening to a tape can always slow the tape, but a secretary taking dictation in the same room cannot. Remember to adjust your speed. Do not look at the person taking dictation or you will speak too slowly.

3   Before you begin the text explain whether it will be a letter, a memorandum or some other format. Specify the layout if it is in any way different from usual. Say how many copies are required, what heading is to appear and what sort of paper should be used. If the context does not make it clear, clarify who should receive copies of the document. If dictating on to tape it might also be helpful to give your typist some idea of the length.

4   Spell out unfamiliar or difficult names.

5   Specify the punctuation. Indicate where there should be commas, colons and full stops. Do not suddenly inform your listener that you

have come to the end of a quotation; begin the quotation by saying 'open quotes' or 'inverted commas'.

6   If your secretary is working on a word processor you can ask the secretary to move, insert or delete material. But this can be confusing. By all means dictate your second thoughts, but be clear and do not overdo it.

# 3

## ─────── EDITING ───────

## ─────── **The whole document** ───────

All authorities on writing advise that after drawing up your first draft you should put your draft aside for a while (an hour, a few days, a few weeks, depending on your schedule) before making further changes. There are two valuable advantages to doing this. First, it often happens that when you turn your conscious mind to other activities, your subconscious mind becomes free to mull over what you have written and make connections between facts and ideas you had not consciously thought of. Second, taking a break enables you to return to your draft with a fresh mind, with a better chance of noticing what it is you have said or not said rather than what you thought you were saying. In other words, returning after a break helps you see what needs to be moved, what needs to be added and what needs to be taken out. This is what editing is all about.

Now that so many people produce their work on word processors, changing the text has become much easier. Some people notoriously go wild on their word processors, fiddling aimlessly and endlessly with the text. This chapter can direct you to make your changes purposefully and efficiently.

## Moving material

In your pre-writing stage you planned the order in which you were going to present your material. Now is the time to reconsider that order. Sometimes writing the first draft will uncover problems in organisation that you could not have seen at the outline stage. Maybe, once you see the document as a whole, you realise that a particular fact that you had planned for the middle of the document would instead work more effectively placed at the end to leave the reader with one last, emphatic punch. Try it out. Experiment with the document until you feel satisfied with the order of your material.

## Adding material

We have all suffered the embarrassment of discovering too late that we have omitted some essential detail from a document, such as writing a memorandum announcing a staff meeting that carefully sets out the venue and the agenda but omits the time. The problem is how to discover what should be there but has been forgotten. Here are two useful techniques.

1   Be absolutely thorough in the pre-writing stage and be sure to think of all the possibilities. Put yourself in the place of your reader and imagine everything the reader needs to know. (See pages 9–15.) But even this precaution is not error-proof; you know from experience how easy it is to think you have covered all necessary points but still, no matter how often you have gone over something, to miss one important detail. And even if you had the ability to be fully comprehensive, you do not always have the time. How then can you discover what you forgot at the pre-writing stage?

2   Have someone else go over your document in the hope that the omission *you* could not spot would be obvious to the other person. Of course if you're going to ask someone else to look over the document you should be very careful to choose the right person. Do not look for someone who will always agree with you or you will receive the unhelpful reply that the document is fine, 'a super job, CJ'. On the other hand, do not choose someone who is overly critical unless you can be sure you will not lose your temper or bear a grudge. You are

letting this person see the document before it is polished; do you want it to be seen in this state by that person?

Do not forget too that the person looking over the document should know something about your subject and about your audience or else what is the point? At a later stage, when you want to be sure your sentences and diction are clear it may be useful to have someone read the document who is not familiar with the subject, but when editing the document as a whole you need a knowledgeable reader.

Probably the ideal person for this job is your assistant. If your assistant is also the person who types out the final draft of most of your work, then he or she will know better than anyone else what your work should be like and will provide the fresh perspective that can spot what may have been left out.

But unfortunately we do not all have assistants or even friendly work-mates qualified to read over our drafts. All we can do then is keep our mind very carefully on the reader's needs as we read through the draft at this stage. It may help, in these circumstances, to pretend to be someone else, perhaps an editor. (Here is another example of why even business writing requires imagination.)

## *Deleting material*

It is always easier to take material out than to add it. All it costs is a slight pang to your ego as you throw away a phrase or a paragraph that you may have thought was particularly elegant but that you now see was not really relevant.

Dr Johnson once said: 'Read over your compositions, and wherever you meet a passage which you think is particularly fine, strike it out.' Of course he was exaggerating, but his point was that our liking for a certain passage may encourage us to retain it at all costs, even if it doesn't quite belong. Be alert to where you may be deceiving yourself.

If you have done your pre-writing stage well, you will have a main point that can act as your filter. (See pages 36–7.) Anything in your document that does not directly support your main idea should be filtered out.

## Example

Maybe you are writing a letter to your supplier explaining why your company's payments will be late this month. Your main point may be that because of unavoidable delays in receiving essential parts, your production schedule has been put back, but as soon as the new parts arrive, production can resume and generate the money needed for the payment. Perhaps you explained in your draft that the shipment was delayed because the lorry carrying it had been involved in a 12-vehicle pile-up on the M6 in last week's fog and the parts were smashed when another lorry hit the delivery lorry from the rear. Now, in the editing stage, ask yourself whether these details are essential to your main point. You will probably see that they are off the point. Edit them out.

Another way to test whether something belongs or not is once again to put yourself in your reader's place. You have asked yourself in the pre-writing stage what the reader does not need to know (see pages 9–15); ask yourself the same thing again at this stage. In the example in the box, above, does your reader really care how the delivery was delayed? Does your supplier have the time to think about the accident on the M6?

Reading over your draft you may see some of your material differently from the way you saw it at the planning stage. You may realise that what you had thought was appropriate material is not really suitable for your document and needs to be deleted. A certain topic might seem necessary in your outline, but pursuing it in your draft may lead you to sensitive material that should not go outside your company.

Suppose you are writing up minutes of an especially heated internal meeting on policy towards a certain client. When writing the draft it might have seemed right to include all the details of the debate, but while editing you see how sensitive and unnecessary the details are and delete them.

## *Supplying examples*

When editing your work you should read the draft over once just to see whether you have provided enough examples. Not all kinds of business writing need examples, but in many cases the presence or absence of examples makes the difference between a document that clearly, vividly and convincingly makes its point and one that merely goes through the motions of making a point.

Let's say you are a sales representative for a manufacturer of middle-market women's dresses and are writing up a report about your visit last week to the district manager of a large chain of clothes shops. You must explain that the chain has recently decided to move into a more expensive range of women's wear. You could write that your company should plan to sell the more expensive line of dresses to this chain and cut back on the less expensive line. This sentence supports your main point (maybe it *is* your main point) but does it express precisely what you are advising? Give examples. Which particular dresses would be suitable? which unsuitable? Then your reader will have a clear idea of what this chain is actually looking for.

Sometimes, of course, examples are just what you do not want. If the annual report of your electronics company must announce a large loss due to lower sales, do your want to give an example? Do you want to tell your readers that Dave Winterfall in the shipping department left a window open overnight and £20,000 worth of parts were stolen? Do you also want them to know that Susan Slippard misdirected a message from a customer ordering £8,000 of electronic goods? You may have to put these examples in writing at some time (in a detailed memorandum to your manager), but an annual report is not the appropriate place.

If, on the other hand, you have good news to report then you should give examples to show vividly how energetic or competent the company is or to give praise to the people who deserve it.

For further discussion of examples, see page 42.

## Checking facts

Your facts must be clear and accurate. To check if they are clear put yourself again in the place of your reader. Go through your draft checking that every fact is clear and correct.

If you must choose between clarity and accuracy, choose accuracy over clarity if only for legal reasons. But if your material has to be complicated in the interests of accuracy (such as in the fine print of an insurance policy), be aware that some readers will find your facts unclear. Be considerate to these readers by offering (perhaps in the covering letter or note) a telephone number or some other means by which they can find help.

How do you make sure your facts are accurate? If you know you did your pre-writing research thoroughly, then you need not worry about the reliability of the facts, merely about whether you have transcribed them correctly. Take nothing for granted; be aware of the possibility of mistakes. Check your draft against your notes; have someone else read the figures out loud as you keep your eye on the text; double check that the figures are lined up in their correct columns.

## Exercise

Read carefully through the following table, which shows what percentage of the work in a training department each employee performs. Spot the errors.

|  | G Wattan | H Campbell | J White | K Lambbert | L Lambbert |
|---|---|---|---|---|---|
| Assigning staff to external courses | 20% | 60% | 0% | 0% | 0% |
| Designing internal courses | 20% | 0% | 50% | 20% | 20% |
| Assessing need for new courses | 10% | 20% | 20% | 25% | 25% |
| Assessing need for new courses | 25% | 0% | 30% | 25% | 25% |
| Conducting the courses |  | 0% | 0% | 25% | 25% |
| Evaluating courses | 25% | 20% | 0% | 25% | 5% |

# Paragraphs

Paragraphs divide your document into sections that you want your reader to consider as individual units or sub-units. Making good use of paragraphs is a courtesy to your reader.

Every layout editor knows the value of 'white space' on the page, that is the spaces around and between parts of the text. It is much easier on the reader's eyes to read a page that is not a mass of black print. Paragraph breaks create white space; therefore the more frequent the paragraph breaks the easier the page is to read.

Do not let your paragraphs go on too long. Guard against paragraphs that run on for more than one third of an A4 page single-spaced. Such a mass of text will daunt most readers.

The length of your paragraphs can determine the pace of your document. A succession of long paragraphs gives the feel of ponderous, weighty matter; short paragraphs can give the feel of a rapid, hard-hitting business presentation. It is worth trying to vary the length of your paragraphs, though, if only to prevent boredom.

Good paragraphs do more than just comfort your reader's eyes and provide variety. Good paragraphs help you present your argument in a clearly organised, methodical fashion. Each paragraph represents one point or sub-point you wish to make, and proceeding from paragraph to paragraph should enable your readers to follow your argument step by step. But to work effectively in this way your paragraphs must be well organised and coherent.

## Exercise

Break the following unreadable, long paragraph into as many shorter paragraphs as you think suitable.

There are two venues in our town suitable for our company's Christmas lunch – Restorante X or Hotel Y. The two are fairly similar in many respects (location, prestige, parking), but they do differ in cuisine, atmosphere and price, and a comparison along these lines would help make the choice easier.

Ristorante X, as its name suggests, is an Italian restaurant, with a full range of Italian foods and no 'British' items on the menu. Hotel Y, on the other hand, specialises in English cooking. The food there is not unusual but everyone agrees that it is well prepared and attractively presented. The atmosphere at the Ristorante X is very attractive. We could book one of the large rooms off the main dining area where we could make as much noise as we wanted to without disturbing any one else. We could have our choice of different kinds of background music. The only problem is that there are no windows and the ventilation is poor. If several people start smoking it would be sure to spoil the meal for the non-smokers. If we announce no smoking, it may spoil the meal for the smokers. The atmosphere at Hotel Y is, like the cuisine, plain but tasteful. We wouldn't have a room to ourselves, but just an alcove, which, though roomy, has a low ceiling and would therefore be very noisy. Despite the low ceiling, however, there is a good ventilation system, and as long as the smokers sit together at the far end of the alcove, there should be no trouble about smoke. Ristorante X offers a choice of two three-course meals, including one glass of wine, for £15 per head. Hotel Y offers a choice of four three-course meals (including a salad bar) for £12 per head. Given the fact that many people at last year's party complained of the 'foreign' food and that tension at the office between smokers and non-smokers is running high, and since there are many people who wouldn't want wine and would resent paying for it as part of the meal, it seems obvious that we should choose Hotel Y for the Christmas party.

## The well-organised paragraph

Organising a paragraph is like organising a document as a whole: you need to introduce your material, support it and, often, draw conclusions upon it. A good paragraph should contain four parts: a transition, a topic sentence, supporting details and an ending.

## Transition

A transition connects the paragraph with the previous paragraph. It may be a simple word or phrase such as *next* or *the second step*. It may be a full sentence such as:

> *Despite the financial disadvantages of changing our hours of business a change will prove beneficial in the long run for morale and customer satisfaction.*

This sentence links the previous paragraph, which spoke of the financial disadvantages, and the present paragraph, which speaks of the long-term benefits. In business documents the headings and sub-headings often take the place of transitions as signals telling the reader what comes next.

## Topic sentence

The topic sentence states the main point of the paragraph. Usually it is the opening sentence of the paragraph, in which case the paragraph begins forcefully and then explains the point. It may come near the end, in which case the details in the paragraph build up to a final point.

## Supporting details

Concrete details, explanations or arguments form the supporting details that develop the idea presented in the topic sentence.

## Ending

Some paragraphs look ahead to the following paragraph. Some paragraphs connect the material to the main point of the document. And some paragraphs just end.

Of course, for particular effect, you could have a paragraph that consisted of only one sentence.

## *Correcting problem paragraphs*

At the editing stage you should examine each paragraph to see if it contains a topic sentence, either stated or implied. If you cannot find a topic sentence, your paragraph probably suffers from one of the following problems.

1   The paragraph may contain too much unrelated data. If so, either look harder to see if there is some way to connect the data (and the sentence that expresses the connection will be your topic sentence). Or divide the paragraph into two separate paragraphs, each with its individual topic sentence.

It would be hard to discover a clear topic sentence in a paragraph that speaks first of the need for closer co-operation between managers and secretaries and then of a recent decline in sales. After thinking again about this material you might see a connection that had been hidden before:

> *If managers and secretaries co-operated more closely, we'd be able to reverse the recent decline in sales;*

or,

> *The recent decline in sales results from a lack of communication between managers and secretaries.*

Now look over the rest of the paragraph to see that all the details develop this connection. If, in fact, these connections are not what you meant to say and the two points are unrelated, give each one its own paragraph.

2   The paragraph may simply list data without giving them any shape. Some writers think it is their job simply to provide quantities of information. The truth is, though, that unorganised facts are worthless in themselves. They become useful only when given a shape, which means only when they are mustered in support of an idea. The topic sentence is the idea that shapes these facts, and so if you can find no topic sentence for your paragraph, begin to suspect that you are doing nothing but listing facts.

Sometimes the problem turns out to be a symptom of not having thought out your ideas sufficiently in the pre-writing stage. Do more thinking now. Review the facts in the paragraph to see their relationship to the rest of your document. Their relationship might be the idea you are looking for to provide the topic sentence. If you can find no relationship, it is best to omit the material altogether. If you think the material is essential to the document relegate it to an appendix, often a useful storage place for mere facts.

## *Coherent paragraphs*

Just as we need transitions to join one paragraph to another, so we need other transitions to join together the elements within a paragraph so the reader can understand how they fit together. Readers quickly lose patience when they read choppy paragraphs where the sentences do not move easily from one to the next. Such paragraphs ask the readers to do the work of linking one sentence within the paragraph to the next sentence, but it is bad policy to make your readers do more work than necessary. Besides, you do not want to take the risk that in providing the links themselves, the readers might provide the wrong links and misunderstand you. Incoherent writing is not only annoying but potentially misleading.

When editing your paragraphs draw upon these four ways of strengthening coherence.

### Using transitional words or phrases

Internal transitions (whether single words or phrases) can show the relationship between sentences. If you have understood the organisation of your paragraph then presumably you can tell your reader how any sentence relates to the sentences before and after it. The various kinds of relationships and some transitional words and phrases that express these relationships are listed below.

| | |
|---|---|
| **Example** | |
| for example | that is |
| for instance | such as |
| **Cause** | |
| because | given that |
| since | on account of |
| so that | due to |
| in order to | owing to |
| for this reason | |
| **Effect** | |
| as a result | thus |
| therefore | consequently |

## Time

next

then

subsequently

before

after

meanwhile

at the same time

later

previously

finally

first, second, third . . . at last

## Comparison

similarly

in the same way

likewise

## Contrast

on the other hand

but

although

however

by comparison

in contrast to

nevertheless

on the contrary

alternatively

## Addition

also

too

as well

as well as

in addition to

besides

furthermore

moreover

again

next

first, second, third . . .

## Repetition

in other words

that is

again

in brief

as I said

as we saw (above)

## Conclusion

thus

in conclusion

therefore

as a result

consequently

## Summary

in brief

to sum up

in other words

in summary

## Relating old to new material

Another way to link a sentence to the previous one is by referring to something that was said in the previous sentence. This is best explained through examples. Consider these two sentences:

1  The Planning Authority has given permission for a new housing estate at the end of the road.

2  The residents are distressed and are planning to mount a campaign.

We can guess the relationship between these two sentences, but we would only be guessing and we might in any case resent that the writer made us do the work. How much more coherent, and therefore clearer, is it to tie the sentences together in this way:

1  The Planning Authority has given permission for a new housing estate at the end of the road.

2  The residents are distressed *by this decision* and are planning to mount a campaign *to have the decision overturned.*

Notice the way the italicised phrases link the two sentences by referring to material in the first sentence.

Consider another pair of sentences:

1  The sales rep, who has a company car, claimed £200 in expenses for taxi fares.

2  The accountants refused to allow these expenses.

It is possible that we do not care why the accountants refused the expenses, but in most cases it would be important to understand the cause of their refusal. Perhaps rather than adding more material to the second sentence we need to introduce a third sentence to clarify the causal relationship:

1  The sales rep, who has a company car, claimed £200 in expenses for taxi fares.

2  Company policy states that no one having use of a company car can claim for taxi fares.

3  The accountants refused to allow these expenses.

## Keeping the outline of the paragraph in your reader's mind

Use transitions as guidelines so the reader can keep in mind the pattern of the paragraph. Sometimes you may feel that you are stating the obvious and that too many transitions make your writing too simplistic and unprofessional. In fact your reader will be grateful for being able to follow your argument easily. Notice the way transitions in the following paragraph keep the pattern in the reader's mind:

> *There are three reasons for shopping at a corner shop. First of all, you get personal attention. Second, you are supporting a local business. Finally, you can shop there without causing pollution from driving your car.*

## Repeating key words

Many people try to avoid repeating the same word several times in a paragraph. This obsession with not repeating words probably arises from some vague memory of a teacher who, to encourage pupils to increase their vocabulary, forbade the use of the same word twice. But as a device for helping your paragraph cohere, repetition is very useful. Repeating *non-key words* will be distracting and annoying, and will signal to your reader that your vocabulary is limited. But never be afraid to repeat *key words*.

Watch how the repetition of 'footpath' and 'kerb' helps bind the material together in the following paragraph:

> *The new road layout pays particular attention to pedestrian safety. The eastern footpath will remain next to the road, but we will lay the footpath 75mm above the road surface. There will also be a series of yellow lines next to the footpath, to delineate the kerb to both motorists and pedestrians. On that kerb there will be an area of lower kerbing to assist pedestrians crossing with prams and wheelchairs.*

# Sentences

When you write your first draft it is best not to think very much about the kind of sentences you are producing; it is hard enough to get the ideas down on the page in the first place. Now, at the editing stage, you have to go back and strengthen your sentences. Even the best writers do this. Or perhaps we should say *especially* the best writers do this.

In fact the best writers do what many less confident writers prefer to skip: they scrutinise each sentence to ensure that it says all it needs to say and no more in the most effective way. This chapter will help you understand what is the most effective way to shape a sentence so that you too will have the confidence to examine and improve each sentence in your draft.

An initial hurdle that daunts many people at this stage is their unfamiliarity with grammatical terms. To speak clearly about sentences, we have to make use of semi-technical terms such as *subjects, verbs, phrases* and *clauses*. Familiarity with these terms is not essential to understanding the following pages, but it will help.

The scope of this book does not include a review of grammatical terminology, but if you feel you need some revision, or would like a handbook to guide you as you consider sentences, there are many books on the market, such as the two in the *Teach Yourself* series, *Correct English* and *English Grammar*, both by B. A. Phythian.

## *The heart of the sentence*

At the heart of any sentence is the subject, the verb and, if present, the direct object or the subject complement. The first step in strengthening sentences is to recognise the heart of the sentence so you can then determine whether the main point of the sentence is found at the heart or has been left on the edge somewhere.

Remember: every sentence has a subject and a verb. The subject is the person or thing performing the action. The verb is the action. A basic sentence, therefore, could be,

*The chairman spoke.*

*Chairman* is the subject; *spoke* is the verb.

Just be aware that not all verbs describe as clear-cut an action as *run*. The chairman could also *think, receive* or *sleep* and these are all technically actions.

To reach the heart of a sentence, first eliminate any prepositional phrases, adjectives, adverbs, articles or other modifiers. Then identify and underline the verb twice and the subject once (it is usually easier to identify the verb first and then the subject). Here are a few examples.

~~The~~ fire raged ~~all night in the abandoned factory~~.

~~After the fire inspector's investigation competent~~ demolition workers ~~quickly~~ pulled down the shell ~~of the building~~.

~~The dirty~~ pile ~~of charred timber and bricks~~ lay ~~on the site next to the railway lines for six months~~.

We would probably agree that the most important items in these three sentences appear at the heart: *fire raged; demolition workers pulled (down) shell; pile lay.*

Now consider the following sentences, where the important items are not at the heart:

I refer to your letter of 12th April concerning your purchase of our deluxe garden furniture suite.

Before considering your complaint, it is necessary for me to clear up one or two points about the sale.

The difficulty about the present condition of the furniture depends upon knowing the person authorised to transport the furniture to your house.

Was it your choice to take the furniture away with you on the day or to have us deliver the furniture later in the week?

These sentences are ineffective. Nothing important to the message appears at the heart of these four sentences: *I refer*; *it is necessary*; *difficulty depends*; and *was it choice*. The message may be getting across, but only in a weak way. How then can we strengthen these sentences?

One mistake many people make at this stage is to stare at the sentence looking for places to make adjustments. It is better once you recognise that your sentences are weak to move away from the sentences back to your ideas. Your new sentences will probably look entirely different from the first version, and they will almost certainly be stronger.

Try to list the basic elements of your message:

You have a complaint about furniture.
I need to know who brought the furniture to your house.

Now we can construct new sentences, with these elements firmly at the heart.

<u>I</u> <u>have received</u> your complaint about the garden furniture suite that <u>you</u> <u>bought</u> from us on 12th April.
Before considering the complaint, however, <u>I</u> <u>need</u> to know whether <u>you</u> <u>brought</u> the furniture home yourself or <u>we</u> <u>delivered</u> it.

## Co-ordination and subordination

The sentences in the original draft of the letter answering the complaint about the garden furniture were **simple sentences**, that is, they contained only one clause. They had only one set of subjects and verbs: *I refer*; *it is necessary*; *was it choice*; and *difficulty depends*. A simple sentence can be very effective in stating directly a single important point.

Sometimes we need to state more than one point in a sentence, as in the edited version above where the two sentences contain more than one clause: *I have received . . . complaint* and *you bought* in the first sentence, and *I need to know, you brought . . . furniture* and *we delivered it* in the second sentence. Sentences with more than one clause are either **compound** or **complex sentences**.

**Compound sentences** contain two or more clauses joined either by a semicolon or a co-ordinating conjunction (*and, but, or, nor, yet, for* or *so*). The clauses in a compound sentence are co-ordinate, of equal importance. This kind of sentence is useful, for instance, when offering a balance of alternatives,

*You can work from 8.00 to 4.00 and Bill can sleep from 10.00 to 6.00.*

Here there are two clauses each containing a subject and a verb (*you can work. . .* and *Bill can sleep . . .*).

**Complex sentences** contain two or more clauses joined by a subordinating conjunction (see list in box below). One clause is the main clause and conveys the main message, while the other clause or clauses modify the main clause in some way. We can turn the sentence above into a complex sentence by saying,

*You can work from 8.00 to 4.00 so Bill can sleep from 10.00 to 6.00.*

Here the first clause (*you can work . . .*) is the main clause and the second (*so Bill can sleep . . .*) is the subordinate clause.

| Most common subordinating conjunctions | | | |
|---|---|---|---|
| after | because | that | whenever |
| although | before | though | where |
| as | if | unless | wherever |
| as if | since | until | whether |
| as though | so that | when | while |

In most cases, complex sentences are more effective than compound sentences or a string of simple sentences. By subordinating one clause to another, complex sentences help the reader distinguish primary ideas from secondary points and the various subordinating conjunctions provide clear indicators of the relationship between the main ideas and the subordinate points.

The effectiveness of complex sentences can best be understood through examples. First, let's look at a series of simple sentences.

- James Tomlinson walked through the building site.
- The supervisor pointed out the various pieces of equipment on the site.
- The supervisor explained his problem with the equipment.
- The problem was causing a serious delay.
- The equipment had not been properly co-ordinated.
- The equipment did not mesh.
- The situation was clear to James Tomlinson.
- The building would not be completed in time.
- Now James Tomlinson could write his report.

The information we need can be found in these sentences, but how easy is it to read and understand them? It is, first of all, hard on the reader to be faced with an unrelenting barrage of simple sentences. Many words are repeated and the relationship between the sentences is often unstated. No one could read this kind of writing for long.

What happens if we combine some of the co-ordinate clauses into compound sentences?

- James Tomlinson walked through the building site and the supervisor pointed out the various pieces of equipment on the site.
- He explained his problem with the equipment and the problem was causing a serious delay.
- The equipment had not been properly co-ordinated and it did not mesh.
- The situation was clear and now James Tomlinson could write his report.
- The building would not be completed in time.

Now the sentences are a little easier to read since related clauses can be found joined in the same sentences. But the passage is still simply a list of co-ordinate points and we have to do the job of sorting out which are the main points and which the minor ones.

Look how much sharper the passage becomes once we subordinate minor points to major points:

- As James Tomlinson walked through the building site the supervisor pointed out the various pieces of equipment on the site.
- The supervisor explained his problem with the equipment, which was causing a serious delay.
- Because the equipment had not been properly co-ordinated it did not mesh.
- Because the situation was clear, James Tomlinson could write his report.
- The building would not be completed in time.

Notice how tight these sentences are, how they avoid unnecessary repetition and most of all how they distinguish between main ideas and subordinate ones. The reader has a much easier job now. Notice too how effective the final, simple sentence is, coming after several complex sentences.

There are other techniques for subordinating besides using subordinate clauses. You can achieve even tighter subordination by using phrases instead of clauses. Both of the following sentences contain subordination but the second one is more concise and therefore probably more effective.

- The two dozen wheelbarrows, which were delivered by rail, arrived too late for the sale.
- The two dozen wheelbarrows, delivered by rail, arrived too late for the sale.

The first sentence is complex; the second is simple. Here is a case where a simple sentence is more effective (because less wordy) than a complex sentence.

## Exercises

Edit these groups of simple and compound sentences to show effective subordination.

1 I visited your house in Bentford Road one day last week. I noticed that the windows and doors need painting; I wondered if you have considered having them painted soon. Painting would keep the premises in a nice and neat condition. I would like to put a tender in for painting the house.

2 Our Company is expanding into your area. We are looking for a few suitable properties needing new doors and windows. We would then install our Snug-Fit range of windows and doors into these properties. We would want to display our advertising board on these properties for a short period of time. We would also want to take before and after photographs of the installation to show the improvements made.

# *Errors to avoid*

Important as it is to write strong, direct sentences, you can destroy the effect of your sentences if you do not know how to correct mistakes in them. Here are some ways to correct your sentence structure. For a more extended discussion, consult a handbook of good English.

## Incomplete sentences

A sentence, as we have seen, consists essentially of a subject and verb. Without one or the other, there is only a phrase, a group of words, not a sentence. We often use incomplete sentences in speech: 'Not on your life!'; 'Where have you been?'; 'To buy some fruit for lunch'; 'Good to see you'; 'Makes me sick!' But unless you deliberately want the effect of a colloquial style (see page 60) avoid incomplete sentences in writing.

Recently the head of a school sent the following notice to her teachers:

*There are certain qualities we expect to see in the teachers working in this school. They must be aware of any unusual circumstances in their pupils' home life that might affect their performance in school. Able to supervise children at play. Willing to take on extra duties. Prepared to coach one sport a term.*

The last three 'sentences' are not sentences at all and it is an uncomfortable struggle to read them. There are two ways the head could have corrected these incomplete sentences. She could have turned them into complete sentences by adding subjects and verbs.

*There are certain qualities we expect to see in the teachers working in this school. They must be aware of any unusual circumstances in their pupils' home life that might affect their performance in school. <u>They must be</u> able to supervise children at play. <u>They must be</u> willing to take on extra duties. Finally <u>they must be</u> prepared to coach one sport a term.*

Or better yet, turn the final three sentences into one:

*<u>They must be</u> able to supervise children at play, <u>be</u> willing to take on extra duties and <u>be</u> prepared to coach one sport a term.*

Another way to correct the document is to set your phrases in a list. Then you can highlight each phrase with a bullet point or some other symbol.

*There are certain qualities we expect to see in the teachers working in this school. Teachers must be:*

- *aware of any unusual circumstances in their pupils' home life that might affect their performance in school;*
- *able to supervise children at play;*
- *willing to take on extra duties; and*
- *prepared to coach one sport a term.*

This sentence provides a useful format whenever you have lists since it helps the reader see clearly each item on your list. Adding a symbol such as a box, a bullet point, a hyphen or a number delineates each item further.

Do not add too many items to your list or by the time they finish the list your readers may have forgotten what you were talking about in the first place. Also try not to have each item take up more than a line or two.

If you want to preserve the clarity of your list, you must keep the items in your list parallel (see below). Notice that each of the bullet points above is followed by an adjective: *aware, able, willing* and *prepared*.

## Faulty parallelism

If you are presenting a series or list of things it is only logical that you present all the items in the series or list in a uniform way. Do not have one item begin with a verb and another with an adjective. Have each one begin with a verb or with an adjective. Similarly do not make one item in the list a phrase and another a complete sentence. Here is a simple example of a faulty list.

### Security checklist

If you are the last person out of the office at night:
- close all windows;
- notify security at the front door that you are leaving;
- the answerphone should be switched on;
- you should check that there are no documents lying around on anyone's desk;
- the lights should be turned out;
- lock the door behind you.

These six items are written in three different grammatical structures. There is the direct command (*close all windows, notify security* and *lock the door*), there is a passive sentence (*the lights should be turned out*) and there is a direct sentence (*You should check . . .*).

The differences do not really obscure the message, but it is easier to take in the message and to see at a glance that there are six steps to be taken if all six steps appear in the same grammatical structure. It takes extra work for the reader's mind to absorb a list that switches between different structures. And some readers will be offended by the faulty grammar, which reduces the message's authority.

It does not really matter which structure you choose for the six items, although the command is the shortest and most direct.

---

### Security checklist

If you are the last person out of the office at night:

- close all windows;
- notify security at the front door that you are leaving;
- switch on the answerphone;
- check that there are no documents lying around on anyone's desk;
- turn the lights out;
- lock the door behind you.

---

## Passive sentences

A passive sentence is one in which the subject *receives* the action rather than performs the action. The person or thing that does the action in a passive sentence is expressed in a phrase beginning with *by* (The book was read *by the student.*), though often this phrase can be omitted. You can recognise a passive sentence because the verb is always some combination of the verb *to be* (*am, is, are, was were, will be, has been*, etc.) and the past participle (*broken, observed, seen, noticed*, etc.).

You can get a feel for identifying the difference between the active and the passive by studying the following sentences.

| Active | Passive |
|---|---|
| The supervisor ordered the new equipment. | The new equipment was ordered by the supervisor. |
| The police opened the door of the flat. | The door of the flat was opened by the police. |
| I understand the instructions. | The instructions are understood. |
| We will audit your department. | Your department will be audited. |

A passive sentence is useful when the agent of the action is not important. It is often preferable to say,

*The milk was delivered.*

rather than,

*The milkman delivered the milk.*

since most of the time all we are concerned with is whether the milk is on the doorstep, not with how it got there.

The problem arises when people use the passive ambiguously. Instead of saying,

*Two boys broke into the shop last night.*

a careless writer might simply say,

*The shop was broken into last night.*

The second sentence would not be very useful to the person responsible for investigating the incident.

Even worse are those occasions when writers use the passive to evade the issue. Instead of saying,

*I broke the window this morning.*

some writers might be tempted to say,

*The window was broken this morning.*

Thus they use the passive to cover up for themselves.

For further discussion of the effect of passives on style, see page 58.

## Diction

After you have edited your document as a whole, adjusted your paragraphs and strengthened your sentences it is time for the last editing stage, reviewing your diction and your choice of words. At this stage you review your document once more, attending specifically to the individual words, checking that they are *accurate*, and where necessary *concrete* and *specific*.

## Accurate words

Are you saying exactly what you mean? Many words refer to similar but not quite identical things and it is important not to confuse them. Have you used the word 'wheel', for instance, when you meant 'tyre'? Have you said 'solder' instead of 'weld'? The only sure way to catch these mistakes is to know your subject well, including the proper terminology, and to read over your draft slowly, keeping your mind alert and critical at all times.

## Concrete and abstract words

Concrete words are those that appeal to one of the senses: sight, sound, smell, taste, and feel or texture. The opposite of concrete are abstract words, which describe ideas or concepts. We need both concrete and abstract words since most writing deals with both objects or people in the world around us and ideas about those objects or people. The topic sentence of a paragraph is often abstract since it proposes the idea to be developed in the paragraph. The details in the paragraph should be concrete to offer a vivid picture supporting this idea.

Sometimes, however, it might be inappropriate (e.g. for political reasons) to be too vivid and your most tactful course is to be deliberately vague. In his famous essay 'Politics and the English Language', George Orwell remarked on the way politicians use fuzzy abstractions to avoid conveying clear pictures. A term such as 'urban crime' is impossible to visualise concretely. It would be much clearer to describe the details of burglaries, muggings, rapes, etc., but in a 'polite' society your reader may prefer not to attend to such things. In such a case you might omit a concrete description to accommodate your readers' tastes. But if you do so make a *conscious* decision to omit it. Do not be content with vagueness.

One of the best ways to achieve concrete language is to draw upon a strong vocabulary. A word like *move* does not conjure up a very vivid image. Picture in your mind what kind of movement you mean and then make the effort to find the right word. Is this movement a *jump*? a *spring*? a *crawl*? a *roll*?

## Specific words

Business writing often proves ineffective because the writer has not taken enough care to find precise, specific words. A writer stating that there had been 'significant improvements in the design of an instrument' has told us nothing. How much better it would be to learn the *specific ways* in which the design of the instrument has improved.

Maybe, though, the writer *wants* to tell us nothing, and would like to leave us with only a vague sense of something good having been done to the instrument. This is the kind of vague, emotional appeal found in advertising: it does not promote clear communication. Intelligent readers find such writing suspicious and lose faith in the writer.

Be on your guard for such vague phrases as *extensive, several* or *considerable* in contexts which require specific quantitative measures. The insurance agent does not want to know that there has been *extensive damage*; state that there was *£30,000 worth of damage*. To say that the repairs will take *several hours* is not helpful for the reader who needs to know when the machinery will be serviceable again; as far as you are able to, give the specific time the repairs will take. Gardeners do not want to know that there will be *a considerable drop in temperature*; they want to know whether a frost is likely or not.

Suppose you run a fish restaurant and are writing a letter of complaint about the excessively long time it has taken Company A to deliver your order. What does 'excessively long time' mean? This general statement is useful, but it needs to be supplemented with an example or two.

How much more effective it is to explain that 'last month's order for 25 gallons of cooking oil was not shipped until the 20th of the month although you had placed your order on the 2nd.' Now your reader can see the problem more clearly and agree that, yes, this *is* an 'excessively long time'.

The effectiveness of an example is directly related to how concrete, vivid or precise it is. 'Cooking oil' is more specific than 'kitchen supplies', for example. In conjunction with your letterhead showing that you run a fish restaurant, it will tell your reader that this is a matter of prime importance to your business. By spelling out the dates precisely, you make the exact length of the delay clear to the reader. The facts speak for themselves.

## Connotation and denotation

Another thing to look out for when editing diction is whether you have used a word with the appropriate connotations. A word's *denotation* is its dictionary meaning; its *connotation* is the shade of meaning it picks up through being used in certain situations. Some words, like *fork* or *hat*, have just a denotative meaning; other words have feelings or associations that make them appropriate in one context but not in another.

Most of us develop a sense of connotations through our ordinary use of the language. Rely on this sense as you edit and be sensitive to words whose denotation may be right but whose connotation makes them feel out of place. *Boss* and *manager*, for instance, both mean the same thing, but would *boss* feel right used in a formal business occasion?

Problems in connotations often arise when people consult a thesaurus to look for synonyms. A thesaurus can provide a list of words with similar denotations, but most thesauruses do not differentiate connotations. Suppose you were writing that a group of politicians ran to the plane and the thesaurus suggested *sprinted* as a synonym for *ran*. Would it be appropriate to say the politicians *sprinted* to the plane? Probably not, since *sprinted* is associated with athletes, not politicians. Do not let the thesaurus take the place of sensitivity to a word's connotations.

# Clichés

A cliché is a word or phrase that was once a colourful or clever expression but has been used so often that no one thinks about its meaning any more. People have only a vague idea of its meaning, and because they know the expression so well, they do not take the time to discover the precise way it is being used. This applies to both writers and readers. Writers like clichés because clichés require no thinking. Writers can just reach for this common expression and give the appearance of saying something. And readers are equally pleased since they too, without having to think precisely, can feel something has been said.

For instance, in speech we might say that a managerial restructuring gave a company a 'new lease of life', but if we are expected to convey precise meanings (as we are in business writing) this cliché will not do. What exactly did the restructuring do? To what extent was the company enabled to resume its business?

To write well you must take the extra time to think precisely what it is you want to say and not to settle for an overused expression. This is not easy; clichés are always clamouring for our attention, but we must resist the temptation and use fresh, honest language.

The only excuses for using clichés are that they can save time and perhaps establish an easy-going, friendly tone. Use them for these reasons if you must, but remember you are sacrificing precision.

# Jargon

Jargon often refers to the technical language employed in a particular field, but in a more specialised sense, jargon refers to the inappropriate use of this technical language. There is nothing wrong with technical language in its place. The problem comes when it is used in a non-specialist context often to impress or overpower the lay reader or to avoid having to think of a more appropriate word or phrase.

If it is any comfort, the use of jargon is not new: in *Gulliver's Travels*, for instance, written in 1726, Jonathan Swift ridiculed the way travel writers tried to impress ordinary readers by loading their descriptions with nautical jargon.

*Finding it was like to overblow, we took in our spritsail, and stood by to hand the foresail; but making foul weather, we looked the guns were all fast, and handed the missen. The ship lay very broad off, so we thought it better spooning before the sea, than trying or hulling.*

Don't be like those travel writers Swift was satirising. Jargon is not the way to cultivate an impressive style. Far from it: at best you will merely look silly; at worst you will antagonise and then lose your reader.

As an example of the way a word can shift from technical language to jargon, consider the word *interface*. It began as a highly specialised technical term in astronomy, referring to the surface forming a common boundary between two parts of matter or space.

Computer experts then adopted the word to refer to a modem that translates the language of one computer into the language of another. Later it came to refer to areas within a computer that interact with each other.

The word next passed into the world of management, marketing and business psychology where it appeared first as a verb meaning to meet or interact with people from different organisations. Then it turned into a noun meaning a meeting or an exchange of information between people from different organisations or parts of an organisation.

Finally it has become jargon, meaning simply any meeting at all. As jargon it is used loosely by people who do not have the vaguest idea of the original meanings. But there are people who still remember the word's meaning in computers or astronomy. To them the word carries the impersonal overtones of something precise, scientific and mechanical. Some people might object to a technical term being used so loosely. Others might object to describing people interacting with other people in mechanical terms.

# Wordiness and pomposity

One of the most common complaints about writing at all levels of business is that it is often too wordy. In an effort to impress the reader, a writer will choose five words where two will do. There is no way to cure this fault except at its root: when that writer learns to appreciate the strength of a direct, honest style, he or she will be able to edit out the wordiness.

Your draft may often contain redundant phrases or loose constructions because your pen (or dictating machine) has run away with you. Scrutinise the wording of every sentence in search of the single appropriate word or phrase in preference to long-winded expressions that play around but never directly hit the point.

Related to wordiness is pomposity. Here writers choose five-syllable words over two-syllable words in the mistaken notion that such words add dignity. Thus we get *individual* instead of *person*, or *finalise* instead of *finish*, *complete* or *end*.

Resist the temptation to inflate your language with long, abstract words. In particular avoid the sing-song effect of a sentence full of *-tion* words:

> *The accumulation of production-related information necessitated the installation of better documentation regulation.*

This sentence cannot be read with ease and the reader can only guess at its meaning. Perhaps it means something like this:

> *Because we have received so many documents about production we need a better filing system.*

# Noun clusters

A noun cluster is a series of nouns strung together to form an almost unreadable and usually vague description of a process or concept. What, for instance, is a 'management recruitment improvement programme'? Is it a programme for improving the recruitment *of* managers, or for improving the recruitment *by* managers? What does an 'electronics management stabilisation programme officer' do?

Usually you can correct a noun cluster by introducing prepositions. Instead of, for instance, a 'bereavement counselling advice centre', speak of a 'centre for advice in bereavement counselling' or perhaps better yet, a 'centre for advice in counselling bereaved people'.

Try to appreciate how awkward noun clusters feel: then you will be able to spot them in your own writing and correct them.

# PART II

# TYPES OF BUSINESS WRITING

# 4

# BUSINESS —— AND TECHNICAL —— REPORTS

Business and technical reports are long, formal accountings. They usually require research, audits, laboratory work, investigations or interviews. They are often the result of a requirement, law, request, demand or expectation on the part of the audience.

Usually reports follow some set and expected format and they include such things as tables, graphs, bar and pie charts or columns of statistics. Compiled in final form by one person, they are often written in sections by different people who report to the final writer or editor.

## ———————————— Purpose ————————————

Reports exist to convey information which will be used to persuade an audience or to make a judgement, form an opinion, urge an action, assess blame or any number of other actions. Each new report is written for a specific purpose, no matter how many similar ones have been written before to the same audience. Despite the fact that a report can 'travel' on from your primary or secondary audience the report is still written initially for a particular audience. (For a discussion of **audience**, see pages 9–15.)

## Content

Each report, whatever the subject, should contain: an **Introduction**, detailing certain preliminary facts about its writing; a **Body**, laying out the situation and presenting findings, results or proposals and perhaps solutions; and a **Conclusion**, summing up what was discussed in the Body and pointing the way to either additional reports or specific **Recommendations** urging a particular action or series of actions.

What follows is a list of the sections of any long formal report. These sections ought to be considered at the pre-writing stage. Some of them you may rule out for a particular report; others you will always include; some you may not have considered. The rest of this chapter discusses each of these sections.

---

This is a list of the basic sections to be included in any report. Consider carefully which ones you should include in each report you write.

*Title Page
*Table of Contents
 Table of Charts and Graphs
 Table of Illustrations (drawings or photographs)
 Summary/Abstract/Executive Summary/Management Summary
*Recommendations (in a list, on a separate page by themselves)
*Introduction (including Purpose, Problem and Scope)
 Background and History (in a separate section if warranted by
    their importance; otherwise this material is covered in the
    Introduction)
*Body
*Conclusion
 Glossary of Terms

---

Bibliography or References
Appendices
Index
\* The items marked with an asterisk should be included in every report.

In shorter reports you may safely omit the separate **Table of Charts and Graphs** and **Illustrations**, the **Summary**, the **Background**, the **Glossary of Terms**, the **Bibliography**, the **Appendices**, and the **Index**.

You need to think in the pre-writing stage about the sections or divisions of your report. Any professional report is designed to be read in sections because not every reader needs to know all the information in the report. Therefore, each reader selects the section most important to that reader's area of responsibility or expertise and reads only that.

The sections also make it easier to read the report and to refer to it in meetings.

**Remember: consideration of your readers' needs is paramount. Realise that the report is being used to glean information, not being read from cover to cover for every fact and statistic in it. Once you absorb that concept and accept it you can begin to think realistically about how to put the report together.**

It is important to divide the report up into logical, coherent, sensible sections or divisions. Spend some time thinking about how you will arrange the report, and how the various subjects within it can be divided. Do not try to include every little fact you have discovered. You may find it fascinating but if your reader does not need it to form an intelligent decision then omit it.

**When in doubt cut it out.**

Remember the report does not have to be written in the same order in which it will be read. You can write each section as you are ready. Each section stands alone and does not have to be tied with transitions to the previous section. A report is not an essay for a tutor at college. You are laying out information which an extremely busy person needs to understand quickly – both the information and its relevance – in order to be able to make a decision affecting the profitability of a company or organisation.

What follows is an explanation of the purpose and content of each of the sections in the list.

## Title page

The Title Page is a separate page enabling the reader to tell at a glance what the report is and who the author is. It should always be on a separate page, no matter how long the report is. Obviously, it should look nice, with a good, clean, crisp layout, with letters large enough to read easily, with lots of white space between the lines. Do not crowd everything on to three lines in the middle of the page.

Do include your name, the name of the report, perhaps the section or department issuing the report, the organisation, the date and perhaps the city or place. You may also want to include the authorising person or department and the funding for the project on the Title Page. It may need to be marked 'Confidential' or have a distribution list attached. Compose this page when you have finished everything else.

## Table of Contents

The Table of Contents lays out the title, headings and subheadings of each section of the report, complete with page numbers listed. Do not omit the page numbers because without them the table is virtually useless.

> You can perform your own check on whether any report is well designed by glancing at the Table of Contents to see if the Recommendations are listed separately. If so, turn to that page and see if they are labelled and written as simple sentences.

After you finish writing all of your report go back over it and assign headings and subheadings to each of the sections, making sure that the heading corresponds to what is covered in that section. Only after you have assigned each heading and subheading can you list them in the Table of Contents with the page numbers. Once the report has been set and paginated you can supply page numbers for the Table of Contents.

You can omit a Table of Contents if the report is of three pages or less.

## Table of Charts and Graphs

The Table of Charts and Graphs lists the names or title of each chart and each graph that you reproduce in the report. This enables the reader to turn to a particular graph to check something. Make sure that the page numbers are also included. Also make sure each chart and each graph has a title corresponding to the material in the chart. Say something about it in your text; do not just insert a graph, expecting your readers to draw the implications or conclusions themselves. You may wish to refer at the base of the graph to a page number for the relevant text.

## Table of Illustrations

The Table of Illustrations contains the titles of drawings, photographs, etchings, etc., as separate from charts and graphs, and the page numbers on which they appear. It is necessary to have this table only if you are using a number of such illustrations.

## Summary/Abstract/Management Summary/Executive Summary

No matter which of these titles you assign it, the Summary should be an accurate outline of what is in the report *including* the Conclusion but *excluding* the Recommendations.

The Summary should be informative. It should not just describe the contents but should tell the reader what the author *says* about the contents. It should not merely list the contents, which unfortunately is what so many summaries do. That happens when they are not properly prepared.

When you have finished writing, edited several drafts, written the Recommendations, inserted the headings and prepared the Table of Contents, read over the report that you have written. (Do not try to remember what you think you have written.) Prepare an outline of it just as if you were reading the report for the first time and were not the author. Write an outline of the report that you have *in fact* written, not of the one you hoped to write, and not following the outline you set up at your pre-writing stage.

When you have edited and double checked your outline, remove all the numbers and letters marking the levels of the outline and simply type it all together with each sentence following the previous one. Finally, you should have a paragraph which is not too long. That is your Summary.

Ideally any Summary is not more than a paragraph long. It should not contain all the detail that is in the report. It is not a substitute for reading the entire report, or even parts of the report. Most people make the mistake when preparing the Summary of trying to put all the information in it that is in the report only in an abbreviated form. That is not necessary.

## Recommendations

Recommendations should be written in short, simple complete sentences, set in a list. They should not go into any detail of justification, persuasion or implementation. They should just be simple sentences compiled in a list.

1   Buy a new XRC machine from International Combination Ltd.
2   Hire a new manager for the division of XRC.
3   Send the 20 staff of XRC division for training in operating the new machine.

Place the Recommendations on a separate page at the front, just after the Table of Contents so that anyone browsing through, scanning or reading the report can find them easily. A manager sitting in a fast-paced meeting should be able to turn quickly to the page with the Recommendations and read them out in the meeting.

**Do not bury the Recommendations on the last page of the report, or in the last paragraph but one. You will only drive your readers to fury if they have to hunt for them. Since they are the single most important part of any report make sure they are easily accessible.**

## Introduction

The Introduction comes just after the Recommendations and before the body of the report. Many readers read only the Recommendations and the Introduction. You should lay out the problem, or the situation, that exists with enough general background information that someone who isn't familiar with it and does not know how the report was commissioned can know what the problem is. It is usually larger than the area covered by the report but it is often just one sentence, especially in a shorter report. It is a good idea to give it the subheading **Problem** so that your readers can locate it easily.

Next you should cover the **Purpose** of the report, that is, the purpose of this particular report and nothing else. Be brief but quite clear about it.

Then you should cover the **Scope**, that is the scope of this report and not of any other report. Perhaps your report covers one area even though there are two other areas readers are interested in obtaining information about. Tell them these areas will be covered in subsequent reports. Give them the author and name and a date of release of the other reports, if you can.

Every report should contain an Introduction, even if it is a single paragraph, which includes these three items, at the very least. You can also add the authorising person, committee or authority, the references you used and any other pertinent information you think the readers might need or want.

## Background and history

Use this section only if you feel the Problem needs much more detail to allow the readers to comprehend what you will be writing about in the body. If there is a long history of a problem pertinent to their understanding of what you will be saying later then expand the Introduction and put it in here. In a very long report (which might become a book) this could be a separate chapter.

## Body

The Body, which forms the bulk of the report, is where you lay out everything you did in the course of your research and investigations, and everything you found. If you interviewed five experts, read ten reports, investigated five alternative sites, ran six special laboratory tests, this is where you tell your reader about them.

Use any or all of the writing patterns discussed on pages 41–56 to show your reader what you have done, what you have discovered and what you think about it. Perhaps you *define* the term you are using or the new concept you are introducing. Then go on to *compare* it with similar concepts used by your audience. Then you might *contrast* it with others to put it in sharper focus for your readers. And finally you offer enough *examples* of what you are talking about so the audience can 'see' just what you mean.

By the time you have put out all this information, using various charts, illustrations etc. as needed, there should be no doubt in your audience's mind what you have discovered. This is the longest section of any report and the place where you spend most of your research and writing time. Be creative. Do not use whatever form your firm has used for decades. Think up a new way to explain the information. Use your brain. Think and rethink ways of presenting the information now that you know how to use the various patterns. Make it interesting.

## Conclusion

Take everything you said in the Body and pull it together in the Conclusion, telling the reader exactly what you think of your material, how you assess it, what you think should be done, which choices should be made, what steps taken, which materials purchased or staff taken on or dismissed. Do not equivocate. Get off the fence. Take a position. You are being paid for your brain and ability to look at data and determine a position. Do not hesitate.

On the other hand, if you know that equivocation is called for, equivocate. Use your discretion.

The Conclusion is also the place, if your firm permits it, to use 'I' because, after all, it is you who have done the research and formed the opinion. If, on the other hand, the work has been done by a team, say 'we' but do not try to side-step your responsibility in this section. Opinion, logically derived from the body of the report, is acceptable here. If in doubt, discuss it with your manager.

When you finish writing the Conclusion write out your page of simple Recommendations in simple sentences. That is the last prose writing of the report. Most important of all move the Recommendations to the front when you put the layout together.

**It is essential that every report you write has a clear and distinct Conclusion section. It is what you are being paid to write; it is the point of all your research.**

### Glossary of Terms

In some long, complicated reports you will be using terms which, although you are familiar and comfortable with them, your audience may not be. In order to save frustration write definitions of the terms in single sentences and list them, alphabetically according to the term, at the back of the report. If you are using electronic, scientific or other highly technical terms it would be an excellent precaution to list them, regardless of what you know about the audience, just on the off-chance that the report might travel on to a less knowledgeable audience, an audience unfamiliar with current terminology in all its intricacies.

### Bibliography or References

List alphabetically by author the names of every book, pamphlet, journal article, other report, etc. which you have used as background material in your report. Include all those you may have quoted from. You might even include interviews. This section lends credibility to your report.

There are many formats for bibliographies. Choose the appropriate one for your field and be consistent. (You can get a good idea of the appropriate format by seeing how recent books and journals in your field present bibliographies.)

### Appendices

An Appendix is an inclusion in your report of other reports or documentation which you want the readers to be able to turn to at will. Appendices also form part of the report in a legal sense if you want to include controversial information which you cannot put into your report in any other way, such as laboratory results from a competitor. You can also use an appendix to bring any other reports to the reader's attention. The appendix can contain information which supports your side of a situation by providing further proof which you didn't want or didn't have space for in the body of the report. Give each item a *title* and a *letter* or *number* by which you list it in the Table of Appendices or Table of Contents.

### Index

An Index is the alphabetical listing of every important name, word, term, concept, item which appears in the report and which someone might want to look up or refer to. It is not the same as a Table of Contents. You might have a separate Index for names and another for places or spaces, or whatever. Many reports are not long enough to need an index but you might on occasion consider using one.

**Note: this list of sections of long reports is suggested as a guideline; however, you will need to amend or add to it sections you find relevant for your company or your work. Your company may refer to these sections by different names. Be creative. Think about what will most help the reader to understand the information you are providing.**

**Remember that you can write these sections in any order in which you obtain the information. You can them put them together later. If you have much of the body before all the data are in, then write it up first. Work in stages because that will be easier. The task will then seem less daunting.**

## ———— Types of Reports ————

The type of report you produce is controlled only by the content. Among others, you can have technical, feasibility, research, personnel, budget, audit, strategy, planning and management reorganisation reports. The beauty of report writing is that it is flexible and adaptable. Use the report to suit what you are doing.

Never forget that a report is supposed to work for you, and for the reader. Do not let the material control you, nor be intimidated by a bulk of research. Grasp it, shape it, do what you need to with it, make it work for your purpose and for your readers. Make it objective and clear and very easy to read. Remember that a report is not a mystery novel: it is not a novel of any kind. It is not fiction. It is the simple straight-forward setting out of what you have discovered and what you think the company should then do. So be very clear about your audience and your purpose before you put pen to paper or finger to keys.

**Be firm. Be clear. Be flexible. Make the Report work for you.**

### Exercise

Take any report from within your company or any other report that you have been given in the past year, and read it critically, examining each of the sections discussed here. Write out a list of the sections used in the report and consider whether or not they fulfil their function.

Then repeat this critique for one of your own reports. Ask a colleague to do it for one of your reports. Pool your information and discuss what you have found. Be critical but positive about your findings.

**Example of report**

BENSLOW LANE, HITCHIN
**Traffic, Access & Development**

A report by Benslow Residents' Group
to
The Inspector appointed by the
Secretary of State for the Environment

DoE ref. no: APP/X1925/A/89/136068

May 1990

1

## CONTENTS

2

## SUMMARY

Mega Builders' two recent revisions to their housing development plans were rejected by the North Hertfordshire District Council on 7 March and 8 May 1990. They are now appealing against these rejections. Mega Builders' development plans, with access via Benslow Lane, will aggravate the already serious traffic condition in the Benslow area. The issue of building a road bridge over the railway needs further study before being dismissed as an alternative to the Benslow Lane access route. Other access possibilities, alternatives to the main junction and a parking ban have been rejected already by the Council.

## RECOMMENDATIONS

The Benslow Residents' Group propose the following recommendations:

1. The Council should dismiss the Appeal by Mega Builder Homes to build 45 houses on Benslow Lane with access via lower Benslow Lane and Highbury Road.

2. Any development at the top of Benslow Lane should have access via a road bridge over the railway to St Michael's Road.

3

1. **INTRODUCTION**

1.1 Problem

North Hertfordshire District Council has refused planning permission, on the grounds of inadequate access and loss of amenity, for a proposed 45-house development (Ref.1/577/88) that would increase residential traffic in the lower part of Benslow Lane by more than a third. The Council has also confirmed its decisions, made in the late 70s and early 80s, that access to the land in question should be via Benslow Lane.

If the prospective developer's appeal against the refusal is upheld, a substantially increased amount of vehicular traffic into and out of the Benslow area will have to pass along a 100-metre stretch of lower Benslow Lane narrowed to a single track by permanent parking on both sides, and immediately adjacent to one of Hitchin's most awkward, congested and hazardous road junctions.

1.2 Purpose

This report sets out the reasons why the proposed development should not go ahead without an alternative access.

1.3 Scope

This report is concerned with the traffic problems connected with the proposed Mega Builders housing development. It does not examine whether the houses should be built but simply what is the best means of access to such houses as may be built.

4

## 2.    **HISTORY AND BACKGROUND**

### 2.1    Description of the Benslow Area

The Benslow Area of Hitchin consists of Benslow Lane, Benslow Rise and Ibberson Way. (See Appendix One for a map of the area.)

The only way for vehicles to enter or leave the area is by Benslow Lane, via the junction with Highbury Road. In effect, the area is a large cul-de-sac, containing 123 houses, four flats, a primary school, a private hospital, two nursing homes and a residential music school. There is a block of five flats under construction. Railway commuters park in the area in some numbers.

### 2.2    Description of Traffic Flow Problems

### 2.2.1    Parking. At its lower end Benslow Lane is 7 metres wide, but its usable width is restricted to approximately 3.8–4.0 metres for a distance of about 100 metres. The terraced houses in this stretch of the lane have no garages or off-street parking, so the residents park their vehicles on both sides of the road. Vehicles are also parked here by residents of Walsworth Road, where on-street parking is not permitted. The number of vehicles parked along this stretch of Benslow Lane sometimes exceeds 50, and is rarely less than 25.

### 2.2.2    Passing Places. As two cars cannot pass in the available width, motorists treat the lower lane as a single-track road with passing places. Passing

5

places are arbitrary gaps in the lines of parked vehicles, whose number, size and spacing depend on the time of day and the day of the week. During working hours on weekdays there are usually plenty of passing places. Outside working hours, and especially at weekends, the lines of parked vehicles are often continuous or nearly continuous.

Passing places are hard for drivers to see until they are close to them, and vehicles will often wait at either end of the congested stretch for an oncoming vehicle that may be seen as much as 150 metres away. There is little alternative to such courtesies. The congestion and delay can be substantial at busy times, which occur regularly on weekdays from 7.45 to 9 am, from 3 to 3.45 pm in termtime, and at irregular intervals later in the afternoon and evening and throughout the weekend. A milk float, a dustcart or a taxi in the congested stretch is often enough to block the Lane completely for a while.

Vehicles are not supposed to park within 30 metres of the junction with Highbury Road. This leaves some room for passing and queuing at the lower end of the single-track stretch of the Lane, and for vehicles waiting to enter Highbury Road. The capacity of this buffer zone is often exceeded at peak traffic times, causing further congestion and delaying vehicles trying to enter or leave Benslow Lane. Vehicle access for the block of 5 flats now under construction is within this zone.

6

**2.2.3** <u>Junction with Highbury Road</u>. The junction of Benslow Lane and Highbury Road is so close to the mini-roundabout at the Highbury/Walsworth/Verulam Road junction that it effectively forms a single 5-way intersection. A zebra crossing traverses Highbury Road between the mini-roundabout and Benslow Lane. There is another zebra crossing round the corner in Walsworth Road, a few metres from the junction.

The motorist emerging from Benslow Lane must take into account vehicles coming down Highbury Road, vehicles turning right from the town centre into Highbury Road, vehicles crossing the junction from Verulam Road, vehicles emerging suddenly from the hidden access from Walsworth Road, and pedestrians at both ends of the intervening pedestrian crossing. This requires particular care even at quiet times; at peak times it is an unpleasant procedure with manifold opportunities for human error.

For vehicles leaving Benslow Lane, the hidden access from Walsworth Road is a serious hazard. Adults and children using the zebra crossing are even worse off, as the eight lines are grossly deficient on both sides of the crossing. In these respects, the whole junction might almost have been designed to test the common sense and quick reactions of pedestrians and motorists alike. Its inadequacies are emphasised by regular minor collisions and innumerable near squeaks. It is fortunate that there have been no serious injury accidents here in recent years.

7

2.2.4    <u>St Andrew's School</u>. In contrast to the awkward
and sometimes overloaded traffic arrangements in
lower Benslow Lane, its middle section is wider
and relatively uncongested. A scene of minor
chaos is enacted twice daily on weekdays in
termtime outside St Andrew's School, as parents'
cars stop and turn in the entrance to Benslow Rise.
In addition commuter parking has increased in
the vicinity of the school since parking charges
were introduced in 1987 at the railway station.

2.2.5    <u>Above the School</u>. Beyond St Andrew's School the
Lane narrows abruptly, losing one of its pave-
ments. Beyond the top entrance to Benslow Rise
both pavements disappear and the Lane continues
between high brick walls to Pinehill Hospital.
After the hospital entrance, the Lane becomes an
unsurfaced track, narrowing to a footpath between hedges, with open areas of ground on either
side. These open areas are the site of the proposed
45-house development by Mega Builders Homes.
The path divides opposite William Ransome
School: to the left is the railway footbridge into St
Michael's Road; to the right there is pedestrian
access to the County Council playing field and to
the houses in Stuart Drive.

2.3      <u>History of Planning Actions</u>

2.3.1    <u>Origins</u>. North Herts District Council decided in
1978 that access to any housing developments
beyond Pinehill Hospital would be via Benslow
Lane. A road bridge across the railway had been
demolished during the electrification of the line a

8

few years earlier, and was replaced by a footbridge. Opportunities existed to introduced new access routes from The Avenue or from Stuart Drive, but in 1981 the Council chose − to the protests of several far-sighted residents − to ratify its policy of access via Benslow Lane.

Mega Builder Homes applied in 1982 for permission to build seven houses beyond Pinehill Hospital. Permission was refused on the grounds that upper Benslow Lane had no pavements and ran too close for safety to the edge of the quarry opposite the hospital.

In 1982 Pinehill Hospital applied for permission to expand, and was turned down on similar grounds.

In 1982 and in 1983 the growing traffic congestion in Benslow Lane was brought to the Council's notice by Benslow residents. The access policy was again ratified.

2.3.2   <u>Development Plans in 1988</u>. Mega Builders sustained their interest in the land beyond the hospital, applying in 1988 to build 45 detached houses there, a much larger development than had previously been sought. The proposed development would increase the amount of residential traffic in the lower Lane by more than one third.

Meanwhile road traffic had increased. The junction with Highbury Road had become more congested, more vehicles were being parked on both

9

sides of lower Benslow Lane outside working hours, and railway commuter parking had begun to spill over from Benslow Rise into the Lane in the vicinity of St Andrew's School.

Benslow residents did not oppose the development itself, in spite of its size. They opposed access to it via Benslow Lane, because it threatened not only to aggravate the traffic problems in the lower Lane, but also to destroy the most attractive features of the upper Lane by pulling down the old brick walls and uprooting many of the largest and most beautiful trees. A wider roadway would encourage higher traffic speeds and increase the risk to children at St Andrew's School.

Residents protested strongly and in large numbers to the Council and its planners. Residents also carried out their own traffic survey, which indicated appreciably higher peak traffic flows than had been reported in a Council survey. Details of surveys are set out in Appendix Three.

2.3.3   Road Bridge. On 7 July 1988 the Council's Highways Committee recommended a reversal of policy, advocating rejection of Mega Builders' planning application on access grounds, asking the County Council to reappraise the traffic problem, and calling for the rebuilding of the road bridge over the railway into St Michael's Road.

The cost of bridge building became a matter of contention. Residents obtained two estimates from specialist engineering contractors, indicat-

10

ing a likely cost of about £0.5 million (see Appendix Two). The County Council had given a figure of more than £1 million to North Herts DC's planners and councillors, but had also written to residents between August and September 1988 with various estimates between £0.2 million and £0.65 million. The County Council does not appear to have obtained costings of any accuracy. It is clear that its estimate of over £1 million is excessive.

2.3.4 <u>Developer's Revised Plans</u>. Although a special meeting of the Development Services Committee on 13 July 1988 restated the Council's policy of access via Benslow Lane, Mega Builders' plans were withdrawn for reconsideration. They were re-submitted in May 1989, after consultation with planning officers and residents, extensively modified in respect of the proposed alterations to the middle and upper sections of the Lane. Most of the old brick walls, and almost all the trees, would be preserved. Traffic calming measures would be taken outside the school and in the upper Lane, with ramps and pinch points to reduce vehicle speeds.

Mega Builders' revised plans offered a more sympathetic approach to conservation and road safety than their original plans, though they made no attempt to deal with the intractable problem of the lower Lane and the junction. The single-lane stretch with its permanent double parking was left alone by the Mega Builders' plan, quite possibly because it was perceived, correctly enough, as a traffic calming measure that was already in place.

11

2.3.5 <u>Response to Revised Plans</u>. On 21 June 1989 the Planning sub-Committee deferred its decision on the application, repeating its request to the County Council for a review of the access problem, and giving its opinion that major highway improvement works would be necessary at the junction of Benslow Lane and Highbury Road before any part of the proposed housing development was begun. The County Surveyor's letter of 24 July 1989 evidently did not satisfy the Planning sub-Committee, which met again on 26 July.

Concerned protest by residents culminated in the presentation of a petition to Councillors attending this meeting, signed by almost every household in the Benslow area.

Planning permission was refused on access grounds, the County Council was once again asked 'to give serious consideration' to the traffic problem and the Development Services Committee was asked to reconsider Council policy on access in view of the growing traffic congestion in lower Benslow Lane.

2.3.6 <u>Mega Builders' Appeal</u>. On 14 September Mega Builders lodged an appeal against the Planning sub-Committee's decision. The Department of the Environment advised that his would take the form of a Public Enquiry.

12

2.3.7  <u>Accident</u> On Friday, 6 October 1989 a five-year-old child was knocked down a car in Benslow Lane, just below the school. He received head injuries and was taken to the Lister Hospital.

2.3.8  <u>Further Revisions of Plans</u> On 7 November the full Control ratified the Development Services Committee's decision on access, but requested that Mega Builders include "suitable alteration" to the Benslow Lane—Highbury Road junction in their plans.

Early in 1990 Mega Builders submitted revised plans to the Council. A mini-roundabout was proposed for the junction, but the plans were otherwise the same as those turned down on 26 July 1989. On 7 March 1990 the Planning sub-Committee rejected these plans, finding that the proposed mini-roundabout offered no worthwhile improvement over the existing layout of the junction.

2.3.9  <u>Additional Accidents</u> On 8 May 1990 a four-year-old child was knocked down by a car in lower Benslow Lane. On 21 May 1990 a mother and child were knocked off a pedal cycle by a car at the mini-roundabout. It is fortunate that there were no injuries in these accidents.

13

## 3. CURRENT TRAFFIC AND ACCESS CONDITIONS

### 3.1 Housing

There is every indication that pressure for new housing in the Home Counties will increase during the coming decade. The DoE's 1985 estimate of the number of new houses required in south-east England by the year 2000 was recently revised upwards from 100,000 to 570,000. Serplan's estimates are higher at 730,000. Hitchin will participate in this growth.

While Benslow residents may not positively welcome this trend, they understand and accept it. Mega Builders' 45 houses will occupy land that has been scheduled for housing development for more than a decade. There has been a substantial increase in the number of houses planned for the site, but the prospect of development has not altered or been seriously contested during this period.

### 3.2 Traffic Growth

In the 12 years since the Local Plan was drawn up, the volume of road traffic, both generally and in Benslow Lane, has increased by more than one third.

According to the DoE's Revised Traffic Growth Factors, published in August 1989, the number of cars on the roads of the Eastern region increased by 46 per cent in the decade to 1990. Projections for further increase in car traffic from 1988 to 2000 ranged from 34 to 53 per cent. This implies a likely

14

total increase ranging from 95 per cent to 120 per cent from 1978 to 2000. These projected increases are confirmed by the daily experience and anxiety of Benslow residents, as they enter and leave the Lane. Year by year the congestion has grown worse and will continue to do so. Within the next ten years, the flow of traffic at the Benslow area's sole point of contact by road with the rest of Hitchin may well be twice what it was in 1978, when the Council's present policy on access was formulated. The extra congestion will be greater still if account is taken of the cars, motorcycles, bicycles, pedestrians and service vehicles generated by adding more than a third to the number of homes in the Benslow area.

North Herts DC, Mega Builders and Benslow residents have counted traffic flows between 0800 and 0900 hrs on weekday mornings in termtime. Table 1 shows the results of surveys conducted by North Herts DC, Mega Builders and Benslow residents.

15

**TABLE 1**   Traffic Flows in Benslow Lane

| SURVEY BY | DATE | | | | NUMBER OF VEHICLES |
|---|---|---|---|---|---|
| | Total two-way traffic flow in lower Benslow Lane, 0800–0900 hrs | | | | |
| North Herts DC | Wed | 26 | May | 1988 | 140 |
| Benslow residents | Tue | 5 | Jul | 1988 | 188 |
| | Mon | 11 | Jul | 1988 | 158 |
| | Tue | 12 | Jul | 1988 | 180 |
| | Fri | 3 | Jul | 1989 | 216 |
| | Fri | 10 | Jul | 1989 | 184 |
| | Sat | 11 | Jul | 1989 | 214 |
| | Mon | 30 | Oct | 1989 | 224 |
| | Tue | 31 | Oct | 1989 | 237 |
| Caloway Transportation (pp Mega Builders) | Tue | 6 | Dec | 1989 | 149 |
| Benslow residents | Tue | 1 | May | 1990 | 202 |
| | Thu | 3 | May | 1990 | 234* |
| | Tue | 15 | May | 1990 | 197 |
| | Thu | 17 | May | 1990 | 196 |

* Local election day (polling station at school, Nursery Department closed)

16

### 3.3   Highbury Road Junction

Between 0800 and 0900 hrs on Tuesday, 5 December 1989, the Mega Builders survey recorded a total of 1,245 vehicle movements, excluding vehicles entering or leaving Benslow Lane, which would otherwise have been counted twice.

During the same period on that day, the five-way junction as a whole saw a total of 2,212 vehicle movements.

These bare figures give only a faint indication of the gauntlet that has to be run at busy times by drivers leaving Benslow Lane and turning across Highbury Road towards the mini-roundabout. They must try to join a much heavier current of traffic without being ill-mannered, causing danger to pedestrians on the zebra crossing, or obstructing vehicles approaching from the mini-roundabout. They must trust to luck that drivers rounding the corner from Walsworth Road will slow down and be alert.

### 3.4   Inadequate Access

If the Benslow area were undeveloped land being laid out for housing, the present road access would not be considered remotely suitable by current planning standards.

Access to more than 120 homes, a school, a hospital, two nursing homes and a residential music school would demand a road at least 6 metres in width, uncluttered by permanent on-street parking, and

17

with adequate sight lines at the junction with its local distributor road. The junction itself would not be sited within 10 metres of another busy four-way junction, with a zebra crossing between the two. Access to individual homes would not be permitted within 20 metres of the junction.

Such a development might be considered too large to be a cul-de-sac. It would certainly be configured to avoid feeding all its traffic towards an already congested town centre.

In addition a single-track road is not expected to carry excess traffic. <u>Residential Roads and Footpaths</u> (DoE/DoT Design Bulletin No.32, HMSO, 1977) Appendix Four, 'Studies of delays to traffic on single-lane carriageways with passing places', summarises the results of computer simulations verified by controlled tests on an experimental roadway. Paragraph four reads:

> Results from the Transport & Road Research Laboratory studies indicate that simply in terms of their capacity for carrying moving traffic, single-lane carriageways, correctly designed, are unlikely to incur significant increases in delay compared with traffic in free-flow conditions, at flow levels of up to 300 vehicles per hour (total two-way).

To apply the results of researches on 'correctly designed' stretches of single-track road, scientifically planned and carefully tested though they are, would be quite inappropriate to the conditions prevailing

18

in lower Benslow Lane. The lower Lane and its junction with Highbury Road are not 'correctly designed'. They have never been designed at all; they have simply happened. They are the inheritance of an earlier era, which was not swamped by traffic of a volume and speed undreamed of at the time they came into being.

The Lane and the junction should not be expected to cope with as much traffic as some new state road fresh from the developer's drawing board.

Because of the cramped configuration of the lower Lane with its awkward junction, the capacity of both Lane and junction is stretched by the traffic it already carries at busy times — no matter what theoretical 'ratio of flow capacity' the science of traffic planning may assign to the junction alone. Nor does the congestion vanish outside peak hours: solid lines of parked vehicles, outside working hours and at weekends, offer few if any passing places even for the lightest two-way traffic.

### 3.5   The Residents' Position

We are, therefore, stuck with what we have got. Much that is less than ideal about the Benslow area also hampers the daily movements of traffic in a thousand other urban settings.

This may be hardly the fault of planning. But it is legitimate to ask that planning, which is a forward-looking exercise, should act with a view to leaving several hundred individual recipients of its services

19

in a position at least no worse than before. The traffic problems of lower Benslow Lane and its junction with Highbury Road are already bad enough: the residents of the area see no sound reason for the planning process to look back to its decisions of a decade ago, while remaining blind to the greater traffic congestion of the present and to the prospect of yet more congestion in future.

4. **ACTIONS IN THE FUTURE**

4.1 Impasses

North Herts DC's committees are at odds with one another, voting both to overturn the Council's access policy and to retain it. The District and County Councils have batted the issue of traffic conditions inconclusively back and forth for two years.

There seems to be little scope for further movements by Mega Builders, who take the view that they have already committed much time and expense to meeting residents' objections, while following Council policy to the letter.

4.2 Railway Bridge

A railway bridge is said by planners and developers to be far too costly to contemplate, even though the cost estimate given by the County to the District has been challenged by residents and shown to be

20

excessive. A bridge remains the most rational solution to the problem. Pedestrian and cycle traffic from the new estate would still be able to use Benslow Lane for journeys to and from the town centre.

By redirecting vehicular traffic, the bridge would avoid a loss of amenity to Benslow residents, and would not penalise residents of Stuart Drive, St Michael's Road, or elsewhere. St Michael's Road offers an uncongested access with clear sight lines. It leads in both directions to well-planned junctions capable of dispersing traffic into the general flow around Hitchin. Its suitability as an alternative access for the Mega Builders development has not been contested by Councillors, planning officers or its own residents.

## 4.3   Other Potential Accesses

Other routes have been considered and rejected. The route from Stuart Drive would simply afflict one more Hitchin primary school with passing traffic, apart from any other political or planning difficulties that might arise. Access across the County Council playing field from the general direction of Wymondley Road is thought impractical.

## 4.4   Junction Alteration

Suggestions for alterations to the junction at the bottom of Benslow Lane have been made with varying degrees of conviction and uniform implausibility. These have included the recently

21

rejected double mini-roundabout, traffic lights and a one-way system using The Avenue and the 'Bumpy Road', a rough track over private ground linking The Avenue with lower Benslow Lane.

A parking ban in the lower Lane would deprive some or all of the present residents of their parking spaces in order to suit the 45 new households at the top of the Lane, all of which would be amply supplied with their own garages and off-street parking. Traffic speeds would be expected to increase unless additional ramps and pinch points were provided. Either way, the parking problem would simply be shifted elsewhere.

4.5   Additional Development

Benslow residents also fear that Mega Builders' proposed 45 additional houses may not be the end of the matter. There is more land earmarked in the Local Plan for housing development. A planning application for 14 houses on land above Little Benslow Hills (the music school) was submitted and withdrawn in 1988. Another two private houses have been built in the area since 1988. There is potential for development at Benslow Nursing Home and at Pinehill Hospital. Hitchin Girls School has the use of the County Council playing field but does not use it: housing development is said to be out of the question, though the field plainly has enormous potential in this respect.

22

## 5.   **Conclusions**

The Benslow residents believe the Appeal by Mega Builders should be dismissed.

If Mega Builders' development goes ahead in its present form, residential traffic in the Benslow area will be increased by more than a third. This will increase congestion to an unacceptable extent at peak hours and at other times in the single-track stretch of lower Benslow Lane, and at the junction with Highbury Road that forms the sole access to the whole area.

The proposed development will remove the option of a rebuilt railway bridge, and the possibility of a new, separate access to housing developments in upper Benslow Lane will be permanently lost.

The three accidents to children that have occurred in the lower Lane or at the junction in the last eight months are a reminder of the risks of creating more traffic in a congested residential road with a primary school and an awkward exit on to a junction with poor sight lines.

There is no indication that Council policy on access will change once the proposed 45 houses are in place. Benslow Lane will continue to be vulnerable to creeping development, each increment too small to merit refusal, all contributing to a needless and wholly unacceptable degree of additional traffic congestion in a road ill-suited to cope with its present volume of traffic, and at one of Hitchin's most

23

awkward, overloaded and hazardous road junctions.

It is a dismal outlook. The residents of the Benslow area look to the Inspector representing the Secretary of State for the Environment to ensure that the local planning process does not remain prisoner to decisions first taken in circumstances now thoroughly outdated, and never properly reconsidered.

24

# 5

## CURRICULUM VITAE

A Curriculum Vitae (CV) sets out the facts of your life that qualify you to perform a particular job. The CV usually describes your education, work experience, publications and any other related activities you might have done or are doing.

## Purpose

Although some people think a well-written CV will persuade a manager to offer them that dream job they have always wanted, its actual purpose is to secure an interview for a job. The CV by itself will not secure a job though it may open the door to the office of the person seeking an employee. Therefore you should not feel that you must explain everything in the CV; the interview would be the time to do that.

# Content

A CV contains all the relevant elements of your life to the present time. It should include these items:

- name, current address, telephone and FAX numbers;
- citizenship (increasingly important with the spread of business across national boundaries);
- personal notes, such as date of birth, marital status, health;
- education, listed in reverse chronological order beginning with your most recent school, college or university and including the degrees or qualifications you obtained from each one;
- employment, listed in reverse chronological order, including at least the name of the company (addresses can be supplied later) and a brief description of your title and duties;
- honours, awards and certificate – if they are relevant to the job you are applying for;
- hobbies and related activities.

Some people feel that their personal details should not be of interest to an employer. These people handle this issue in different ways: some supply the personal details in the interview, reassuring the employer that, for example, children are not going to prevent business travel; others do not supply this information at all, considering it insulting to be asked questions about an area which is their private business and responsibility.

Be sensible in listing your hobbies and related activities. Do not include silly or trivial things. Do not exaggerate either. Do not, for instance, say you enjoy fishing when you have been fishing only twice, many years ago. What would happen if your interviewer turned out to be an avid angler? Try to make your activities stand out. If everyone has been running marathons that year, how special will you sound if you say that you, too, run marathons? Remember that the whole point of this section is that employers like to know that you are a well-rounded person and do not spend all your time at the office.

**Example of Curriculum Vitae of recent graduate**

## TOMPKINS, Sylvia Laura

72A Broad Street
Shefford, Bedfordshire
Tel 0264-815492

Born: 5 June 1971
British citizen; single

**EDUCATION**

<u>1989–1992</u>   Greenwich University (formerly Thames Polytechnic),
School of Land and Construction Management,
Oakfield Lane, Dartford, Kent.
BSc (Hons) ESTATE MANAGEMENT
Dissertation: 'Energy Efficiency, Conservation and
Improvement. A Study of Comparison
between British and Swedish Housing'
Student Member of the R.I.C.S.

<u>My degree course involved these areas of study</u>: Finance (I), Valuations (II/III), Law (II/III), Construction (I), Information Technology (I), Management (I), Economics (I), Land Economics (II/III), Urban Planning (II/III), Property Management (III), Maintenance (II) and History of Buildings (II).

This coursework gave me the opportunity to work in groups and individually on projects, to deadlines, thus strengthening my organisational and leadership qualities. I am familiar with writing reports on WordPerfect 5.1, have used the Harvard Graphics package and participated in oral presentations.

<u>1983–1989</u>   The High School, Bromham Road, Bedford

GCE A Levels
English (C); Mathematics (C); Economics (C)

GCE O Levels
English Language (A), Art (A), Mathematics (B), English Literature (B), French (B), Biology (B), German (C), Physics (C), Chemistry (C), Fashion & Fabrics (C).

## WORK EXPERIENCE
I have had a variety of jobs whilst at school and in vacation periods at university, including as silver service waitress, newsagent's cashier, warehouse sorter and sales assistant at Laura Ashley.

During summer vacations from university I worked as an office administrator in the insurance brokerage department of the RAC, performing basic clerical and accounting duties. I have also worked as a kitchen assistant and part-time cook at a nursing home for the elderly, with the responsibility of preparing supper unaided for more than 30 residents.

## INTERESTS AND POSITIONS OF RESPONSIBILITY
School: I was school representative for Youth Action; Youth Action Volunteer for four years (receiving a Service Prize); Marketing Deputy of a Youth Enterprise Company (gaining a merit in the exam); and a librarian. I also enjoy Ballroom and Latin-American dancing (Popular Dance Test), Judo and Back Diving.
University: As a student I cycled, enjoyed aerobics, swimming and badminton. I travelled for a month in Europe, having previously spent a large part of my life in the Middle East, West Indies and Africa, because of my father's occupation as a Power Station Engineer.
I am also a member of Friends of the Earth and Greenpeace, and sponsor the schooling of a child in Malawi through World Vision, a Christian organisation.

Referees:

| | |
|---|---|
| Mrs P. Martindale | Mr F. Harrison |
| (Employer) | (Lecturer) |
| Fernlawns | School of Land & |
| Haynes |    Construction Management |
| Beds. | Greenwich University |
| Tel. 0243-444555 | Oakfield Lane |
| | Dartford, Kent |
| | DA1 2SZ |
| | Tel. 081-316 9303/4 |

# 6

## ————— INVOICES —————

Any invoice is simply a means of presenting an account to someone from whom you expect payment.

## ————————— **Purpose** —————————

The purpose of an invoice is to ask for money owed to you. A longer-term purpose is to act as a record of money requested for work done or goods sold. From your client's point of view it acts as a record of where money has been spent and for what reason.

The tone of an invoice is impersonal and neutral; you are not trying to be friendly, ingratiating or bullying. You should not use this occasion to make a sales pitch. You simply want to inform.

# Content

An invoice must contain sufficient information to inform the client or customer exactly what is now owing and for what reasons. The following list sets out the minimum that any invoice must contain.

1   Your company's name or if you are self-employed, your name; the name of the person who did the work or made the sale (if relevant); the address and telephone number.

2   The invoice number. This is your number by which the client will refer to the invoice. Some clients also add their own invoice number.

3   If the invoice is for services rendered, a description of the work accomplished, the date, the fee per day, the total fee and any expenses (with receipts). If it is for goods purchased, a description of the goods, the date and place purchased and perhaps the method of delivery of the goods.

4   If the invoice is presented periodically, include the balance unpaid from the last invoice.

5   The terms under which you expect payment, such as within ten days or 30 days.

6   Your VAT registration number, if applicable, and the Tax Point date.

7   Your signature and the date.

## Example of a sample invoice

**Melius Training Services**    **28 Royson Road**

**London**    **SW12 2XX**      **Tel. 071 123 9876**

------------------------------------------------

INVOICE TO:                INVOICE NUMBER: 1077

Belsize Union Gas Ltd

85 Strait Street

Peterborough

Designing and conducting

Time Management training course,

9 - 10 July 19--    at £600 per day for

two days                           £ 1200.00

| Expenses: | British Rail | £45.50 | |
| --- | --- | --- | --- |
| | Taxis | £40.00 | |
| | | ----- | |
| | | | 85.50 |
| | | | ----- |

                     **Total due**           £ 1285.50

Enclosures:   BR receipts

               taxi receipts

Terms:   Payment within 30 days

*E. Lilly*

Elizabeth Lilly

Training consultant

31 July 19–

# 7

## —— INSTRUCTIONS ——

Instructions are orders set out in a clear and logical pattern so that the reader can easily follow them. They are set out in a step-by-step arrangement following the basic order of a process analysis. (See pages 50–4.)

## —————————— Purpose ——————————

The purpose of instructions is to provide very clear directions, to instruct the reader in exactly how to complete, or to reproduce, a particular procedure. In this way they differ from a process analysis, which is written to inform rather than instruct. Instructions can be simply that – instructions; or they can be orders. The difference lies in the tone adopted.

# Types

The variety and range of instructions is infinite. They can be short as in the instructions for putting together a simple cardboard box in which you store supplies for the office, or they can be extremely complicated for pouring concrete to build a new bridge over the River Thames. We all use them, probably without even realising we are doing so. As you leave the office you often leave instructions for your assistant on what to do or how to respond to a particular client or problem.

## Exercise

Think about the last instructions you followed. Who gave them to you? Did you read them or hear them? Did you follow them? How easily? What was their purpose? Did you achieve it?

# Content

What goes into instructions varies enormously but all instructions should include in an introduction a definition of the concept or term. The introduction may need to include some of the following elements:

1 purpose of the instructions;
2 conditions under which they are followed;
3 preparations of materials and equipment prior to use;
4 special skills involved in performing them;
5 special equipment involved in performing them;
6 critical times or signals to watch for.

Follow the basic layout for a process analysis, with a separate list of material and perhaps one for equipment if necessary. Each time you write out instructions you need to consider whether to include any of these elements. Make sure that you number the items in the steps. Think about the sort of paper you print them on, and the type and colour of ink because if they are to be used under adverse conditions you wouldn't want the instructions fading away at a crucial point.

One area that most writers forget to consider is that of idiosyncrasies or warnings. If there are special things to watch out for, particular conditions which can become dangerous (such as using an electric lawn mower in a thunderstorm) you need to tell your readers. If there are special points, or stages in the procedure that are more important than others or mark turning points, your readers need to know.

Consider a book of instructions on maintaining a cottage industry producing home-made jams, preserves and chutneys. Starting such a business from your home might sound attractive, but there are dangers lying in wait for the inexperienced jam maker.

How do you make sure there will be enough pectin in your blackberry and apple jam (since these are plentiful in your garden), because if there is not enough the jam will not set? One secret is to put the pips in a muslin bag, tie them up and include them in the syrup as you boil it. Another trick is to pour a bit of the syrup out into a saucer and if it goes into lines like a wave you know it is ready to pour out and set. Or you can drip it off a spoon. Are these techniques included in your instructions for making jam?

How do your pour the hot syrup into the jars without their cracking? Experienced jam makers would tell you that you put the jars in hot water – not boiling or they will crack – and then set them out on a wooden board, which will absorb some of the heat when you begin to pour the syrup out. Pour only a tiny bit into each jar at a time so that glass can heat up slowly and not crack.

Any instructions for making successful jam should include these warnings and idiosyncrasies; otherwise they would not be very good instructions and your jam-making would fail. Obviously we are not all in the jam-making business, but each process has peculiarities which we may tend to forget when explaining it to others.

When you finish, read the instructions aloud to someone who is not familiar with the procedure in the hope that this person will catch any errors or omissions.

One final check on your instructions: act upon Murphy's Law and assume that if it is possible for someone to go wrong at any stage of the instructions then someone surely will. Try to go wrong at various stages and see whether your instructions anticipate your error and correct you.

**Always double check that your instructions are *in order* and that *each step* is included and that all *danger signs* have been noted.**

## Example of Instructions

INSTRUCTIONS TO FIRE WARDENS AND DEPUTY FIRE
WARDENS FOR SUPERVISING THE EVACUATION OF
THE OFFICE IN THE EVENT OF A FIRE

### Introduction

These instructions are to be followed precisely in the event of a fire in this company. Each of the designated Fire Wardens (or Deputy Fire Wardens) is responsible for seeing that staff and visitors in their office area leave by the Fire Exit.

Read the Instructions now and understand the explanation of each of the steps to be followed. Memorise the steps. The exits are (I) the door to the landing, proceeding down the stairs to the ground floor and (II) the windows along the back of the office which open on to the roof of the ground floor extension.

NOTE: These instructions assume that the Fire Brigade has already been notified.

### List of Steps

When the fire alarm sounds (or some other warning of fire is given) the Fire Warden (or in his/her absence the Deputy Fire Warden) should follow these steps.

1   Assemble everyone, including visitors, in the central office.
2   Close all doors into the central office.
3   Count heads to make sure everyone is present.
4   Check where the fire is located.
5   Decide which exit to use.
6   Keep calm at all times.

7 Tell everyone to begin leaving in an orderly fashion by the designated exit.

8 Remind everyone to meet outside at the assembly point in the car park.

9 Count heads again as everyone leaves through the exit.

10 Shut the window or door behind you as you leave.

11 Count heads again at the assembly point.

## Explanation of Steps

1 Assemble everyone, including visitors, in the central office near one of the designated exits. Exit I is by the stairs, through the door on to the landing. Do not use the lifts in a fire. The stairs are the easiest and quickest way to reach the ground floor and the outside door. Exit II is through the windows at the rear of the office. There is a drop of three feet on to the flat roof of the ground floor extension. Exit II will require more effort for some people. Ask a staff member to help everyone climb through the window. Shorter people will need to be lifted out. You may need to position someone outside on the roof to help.

2 Close all doors into the central office. Ask staff to close the doors as they come in from the other rooms. This will prevent draughts and help to contain the fire. If you smell smoke or see flames underneath a door, do not open the door.

3 Count heads as staff members and visitors fill the central office. Re-count them as everyone assembles by the exit. Make sure everyone is in the office. Do not permit anyone to remain behind in one of the adjacent rooms. Check with staff to see that all visitors are accounted for. If someone is missing be careful about going into the area of the fire to find them. Follow the instructions you will be given in the workshop conducted by the Fire Brigade. Do not risk anyone's life.

4 Check where the fire is located. Someone may know where the fire is located, or you may be able to see or smell the fire by now. Check that the fire is not coming in the exit by the stairs. Carry out this step as you count heads.

5 Decide which exit to use. Plan to use Exit I, the stairs. If the fire is coming in from the stairs, however, close the door to the landing and use Exit II, the windows at the rear of the office. Do

not tell the staff which exit they should use until you have counted heads.

6   Keep calm at all times. Remind everyone to stay calm. You might repeat this advice several times. Even if you do not feel calm yourself, hearing these words will help everyone to remain calm. Remember, hysteria spreads, just as a fire does.

7   Tell everyone to begin leaving in an orderly fashion by the exit you have designated. Tell everyone again to remain calm, not to rush. Reassure everyone that they will get out faster if each person stays calm. Help those who need help. Do not let anyone go back for personal possessions or office materials. Do not attempt to remove any office materials.

8   Remind everyone to meet outside at the assembly point in the car park. Tell them to keep together, to help each other and not to stray away from the group. Do not permit anyone back into the building for any reason.

9   Count heads again as everyone leaves through the exit. Make sure you have accounted for everyone.

10   Shut the window or door behind you as you leave to prevent the fire from spreading.

11   Count heads again at the assembly point. Make sure again that everyone is accounted for and that everyone stays together at the assembly point.

## Conclusion

The more you understand and know these instructions the easier it will be to make sure everyone leaves the building safely in a fire. We will have frequent fire alarms and exercises to practise so everyone should be aware of the procedure. This should make your job easier in the event of a fire.

Reminders in abbreviated form of these steps will be posted beside each of the designated exits.

# 8

## —————— LETTERS ——————

Letters should be direct, crisp business communications from an individual, or a company, to another individual outside the company, or to another company. They are written in an accepted format, although some variations are practised.

## —————— **Purpose** ——————

The purpose of a business letter is to give or receive precise information in as short a form, in as few words, as it is possible to use while providing the required information. The letter is written for a particular, usually single, purpose (such as obtaining a particular piece of information or reminding someone of a meeting date) to a particular, again usually single, audience. Sometimes the purpose may be to persuade or to re-enforce a relationship.

A business letter should not waffle but should come straight to the point. It should never say more than is necessary to convey the message; in other words, it should not offer too many apologies or provide more than just the information requested. If what you want to say is very complex then you should submit a report or set up a meeting, not write a letter.

When we examine closely all the sorts of letters that business can and do write we discover that they have only two real purposes: all letters either give information or request that information be sent back. At the root of every letter is one of these two purposes, although the information given may act to persuade or remind or re-enforce.

# Content

The content of a letter can be varied but it ought to include the following items:

- your address, telephone number and, if appropriate, FAX number, usually already printed on letterhead stationery;
- the date;
- the recipient's name and position in the company and the company's address;
- the recipient's reference number and your reference number if appropriate;
- a subject heading;
- a salutation;
- the body;
- the closing and signature.

**Pay particular attention to the name and position of the person you are writing to. If you misspell the name or use the wrong title your reader will almost certainly catch your mistake and, aware of this one mistake of yours, may look with suspicion on everything else in the rest of the letter.**

The tone of any business letter should be professional and business-like. The style should conform to whatever your company requires. It should always be appropriate to the image your company (or you) want to project to the reader.

To compose a concise and precise letter think about your purpose in writing the letter and the person to whom you are writing it. (Some letters go out to unknown organisations, but in the main we write letters to individuals, not to organisations.) Go back and review the sections on **Purpose** (pages 15–21) and **Audience** (pages 9–15) and then think carefully about exactly what it is you need to accomplish with your letter. Often you will have spoken to the person on the telephone so that the information you supply in your letter is only a reminder of what was said on the telephone.

Sometimes you will be requesting information which the recipient does not want to give or does not expect to be asked for. Make sure you narrow your focus down to exactly what you want and need. Do not add a lot of extra information or detail that is not essential to obtaining what you really need.

**The fault of most letters is that they are too long.**

Most business people receive far too many letters for the time available to read them in one day and if three pages fall out of the envelope the recipient will be put off. So, make life easier for the readers of your letters: keep them short and simple and very much to the point.

If you are like most people you will sometimes have to write letters you have no idea how to start. You may have reviewed your purpose and audience but still feel uneasy about beginnings. The advice given in the chapter on **Rough Drafts** (pages 63–9) will be helpful here. A quick survey of other letters written by people in your company (perhaps to this very person) may also suggest some helpful approaches.

# Types of letters

There are many different types of letters we could list here, but we cannot provide an exhaustive list because everyone would be able to come up with yet another type. So we will confine our list to general types and then you can add more of your own.

# Adjustments

When writing adjustments give your client enough information to make it clear you are changing the invoice or changing the goods or the delivery date or procedure. You need just enough to convince the reader that you are making a change: facts, figures, dates, times, place of delivery, etc. Do not overload the reader with more than is absolutely necessary to accept that you have made the adjustment.

# Complaints

If you are complaining you need to be very clear about the nature of the complaint: what is it about, when did it take place (use inclusive dates, times, etc.), what times were involved, where did it happen? For example, if you were complaining about the cleanliness in a restaurant you might need to state the name and address of the restaurant, the time and date when you ate there, the description of your waiter or waitress, an accurate description of what you ate, how many were in your party, what table you sat at, etc. If you fail to include enough precise detail the manager of the restaurant will not be convinced that your complaint is legitimate.

# Instructions

Sometimes brief instructions, such as how to get to a meeting, are transmitted in a letter. Again it would be essential to give exactly what is needed to get to the location but nothing else. Anything extra would be confusing and instructions need to be clear. See the section on **Instructions** for how to set them up (pages 145–6).

# Inquiries

If you are making an inquiry about information, or perhaps a procedure, you need to be very clear about what you actually need. Do not ask for more than is necessary. Think about what sort of information you need and what you are going to do with it. Cut out anything that is not essential because you will only confuse your recipient, who may then be less likely to provide the information the way you want it.

## Employment

When you write a letter to accompany your CV (see pages 138–41) you are actually asking for an interview, not for a job; therefore, it is important to supply information in the letter that will supplement your CV and create additional interest in seeing you as a possible candidate for the job. The letter should be short but provide enough detail about one or two projects you completed on a previous job that relate to the current job and would possibly interest the person doing the hiring. Find out as much as possible about the company offering the position and choose something you have done that relates to that position. You want to intrigue them enough to invite you in for an interview or for a second visit if you have been once. Sometimes, you may write a letter after an interview providing additional information to interest the person further in you. But remember to keep it short and to the point.

# _____ The order of the information _____ in a letter

If you have to tell someone bad or negative information in a business letter make sure you present the details leading up to the negative decision so that by the time you do tell your correspondent the bad news he or she is prepared for it and sees the reasons. By then your reader will have become at least partially convinced that the bad news is justified. If you spring it on the reader at the beginning, the reader will have no warning of it, will not have the detailed preparation justifying its validity and will probably not read the rest of the letter to obtain the details. But do not leave the negative information until the end of the letter. End the letter with something positive if you can.

Conversely, if you are presenting good news, do it right away.

In each of these letters – and in the others you come up with – it is again crucial that you sit down and analyse the purpose and the audience. If you write before you have done that you will be wasting time. Be clear about what you want the letter to accomplish before you sit down to write and the writing will go much faster.

### Exercise

Cast your mind back to a letter that you have written at work in the past six months and think about its purpose and the audience. Then write a brief outline of what should be covered in the letter and the order in which you should present it. Then go back to the original and see how you have improved and what you have written. It is not necessary actually to rewrite the letter in order to do this exercise.

**Remember: a few minutes spent at the beginning saves hours of agony later on.**

Here is a letter of inquiry, which has been sent as a FAX.

HELLO ANDY

LONG TIME NO SEE!

DO YOU KNOW WHERE WE MIGHT OBTAIN A

STAINLESS STEEL TROLLEY ON WHICH TO MOUNT A

HOT TABLE FOR USE AS A MOBILE BUFFET?


BEST REGARDS,

DAVE

P.S. DO YOU NEED INFO ON OUR NEW LINE OF

REFRIGERATOR UNITS?

Here is an example of a letter of confirmation, which will also serve as a contract.

---

## PRIME WINDOW CONSTRUCTION, LTD
43 Rouncewell Road
Standswell
XX3 2WW

cc J. W. Weyland
   F. O'Connell

Miss D. Fitzhugh                Our ref: GB/AR
Blackwood Windows Ltd
Wood Lane
Brownhill                     7th April 199_
WW2 5XX

Dear Miss Fitzhugh

### Re: Bay Tree Estates, Carlisle

Following our recent conversation and the visit to the above developer by George Lynd and Peter Clarke, I confirm the details of our agreement to supply the following products to Bay Tree Estates:

   15 Cloister 421 Wood Framed, at January 199_ price list;
   20 Cloister 422 Wood Double-framed, at January 199_ price list.

As agreed the windows will be delivered on or before 1st June 199_.

I trust you find this a true reflection of our agreement.

Should you have any questions about this arrangement please do not hesitate to contact me.

Yours sincerely

*George Brown*

George Brown
SALES MANAGER

---

# 9

## MEETING
## NOTES

Meeting notes report the progress of a meeting and stipulate the actions to be taken as a result of the meeting. Another name for them is minutes. Depending on the requirements of the firm or organisation they also provide information on the purpose, place and people who attended. In addition, they can act as a legal record of the meeting for future use in a dispute. They are usually filed in the firm's records and may be referred to later.

## Purpose

The primary purpose of meeting notes is to provide a record. Secondarily, they may be used by the attendees as a reminder of what they are to do following the meeting. They also tell those who did not attend what took place at the meeting. A manager may find meeting notes useful to prod a recalcitrant employee into action. Listing Action Points to be taken by various attendees (or even sometimes by people who could not make it to the meeting) means that the notes act as a spur to get the job done.

# Types

There are only three basic types of minutes or notes of meetings.

1  **Verbatim notes,** such as the Parliamentary records printed in Hansard, record everything that has been said in a meeting or session. Verbatim notes are useful because they are all-inclusive and impartial; they may, however, reveal personal clashes and acrimonious situations that occur in a meeting and that many companies would just as soon not want recorded.

2  **Narrative notes** record how the meeting proceeded, from the beginning to the end, relating how the arguments for specific points went and who argued for what position. The emphasis here is on the details of the arguments for or against specific points in the meeting, but personal attacks can be eliminated. If anyone referred to the issues raised it would be clear who at the meeting stood for what position. A meeting of the board of a company, for example, might need such a complete account of who proposed what issues and who was opposed and why.

3  **Outline notes** provide the briefest account. Outline notes focus on what was decided upon by the meeting as a whole and which person is going to do what before the next meeting date. Since this form is written up as an outline (see pages 38–41) it is much easier to take down and easier to read.

# Content

The content depends very much on which format you choose for your notes.

## Verbatim notes

If required by your company to produce verbatim notes you will find it useful to use a tape recording and then type up the notes from the recording. This, however, can be difficult because often words cannot be heard clearly, or you may be uncertain who was speaking. After editing for misunderstood words and idiosyncrasies of speech you should be able to produce an account of everything that was said at the meeting. Those who want to find out what was *decided* at the meeting, however, will have to read through the entire transcript, extracting as they read the important points made and the decisions reached. It takes much longer to read and extract the relevant information from such verbatim reports.

## Narrative notes

Narratives notes are the most frequently used method of taking notes at a meeting. They are never simply the story of the meeting as told by someone who was there. The secretary sits there and writes down, in some personal shorthand notes, the basic points made by each person at the meeting. (The secretary should not be the person who is chairing the meeting since it is impossible to do a good job of leading a meeting and preparing notes at the same time.) Each speaker is identified. The major points for each argument are listed. Points of agreement are given at the end of each paragraph narrating the progress of the argument; thus it is necessary to read through each paragraph. You may or may not also include the names of the people supposed to carry out whatever action is expected.

In narrative notes, which include the speakers' names, a reader can learn who actually took what position. In some companies it may be important to document this for future reference or even for someone unable to attend the meeting.

The notes are written up in paragraph form, one paragraph per argument, unless the argument goes on and contains many different aspects. Then you would use more paragraphs.

Before writing such notes find out if they are needed or expected. They take time to write up accurately and neatly and editing is necessary to make sure you have stated the nuances correctly. They also take time to read because the reader has to search or the actions voted upon. Often the draft is referred to some of those present for clarification.

**Avoid narrative notes unless specifically asked to produce them.**

## Outline notes

Outline notes can be written down in a basic outline form while you are in the meeting. They require that you listen carefully to what is being decided in the meeting. Do not allow yourself to be side-tracked by the brilliance of an argument being presented.

To follow the discussions intelligently forearm yourself with the purpose of the meeting and the names of those attending. Know as much as you can about the topics under discussion. The agenda will give you an idea in advance of what topics will be covered. Keep your mind clear of personality clashes and side-tracking techniques used by the attendees to make a point in the meeting. It is helpful to ask yourself at each vote 'who does what next?'

If you decide on a specific format for your note-taking before the meeting you will find the note-taking much easier. You might use something like this to help focus your mind:

*(a)*    topic under discussion,
*(b)*    action to be taken,
*(c)*    people supporting an action or voting for it,
*(d)*    person to take the action,
*(e)*    date by which it must be taken,
*(f)*    resolution.

If a specific resolution is passed, ask for a copy of the precise wording.

Here is an example of how you might set up the sheet:

| | |
|---|---|
| Topic: | People supporting or voting for action: |
| Action to be taken: | Person to take action: |
| | Date by which action must be taken: |
| Resolution: | |

Add any other categories relevant to your company and that meeting. If you make yourself a number of sheets like this, then whenever you go into a meeting you will just have to take one and fill it out. This is especially important if you are also a participant in the meeting and do not want to spend a lot of time taking notes. If you know the subject ahead of time and the people who are going to be there you will be better able to concentrate on the action points voted on in the meeting.

# Final form

Find out if your company or organisation has a required format they expect you to use for the finished meeting notes. Is it acceptable to you? Are there changes you would like to make in it? Perhaps you need to discuss this with your manager. Make sure the layout is as clear as it can be. There should be space for some or all of the following items:

- name of meeting;
- purpose of meeting;
- place held;
- date;
- attendees expected;
- attendees actually present;
- apologies for absence;
- agenda (points to be decided upon in the meeting);
- decisions actually decided in the meeting;
- action points stemming from the decisions (with person responsible and date);
- person to be reported to when the action point is completed;
- new business;
- agenda for future meeting;
- date of next meeting;
- your name;
- authorisation as note-taker;
- date notes were compiled and circulated;
- names of people to whom they were circulated.

# 10

## —— MEMORANDUMS ——

A memorandum is a form of written communication used within a company when it is important that there is a written record of the communication. Except for some differences in format and perhaps in tone, a memorandum is just an in-house letter.

## —————— Purpose ——————

The purpose of a memorandum is to convey information of any kind to the employees within a company at any level. It is particularly useful in conveying messages to many employees and in providing a legal record of transactions within a company.

# Contents

There are no guidelines or restrictions about the content of a memorandum other than that it should not contain anything which could be misconstrued or prove embarrassing, especially when uncovered in a file in the future.

Write the memorandum in complete sentences, in appropriate business language and style.

Usually a memorandum is written on a memorandum form with the headings **To:**, **From:**, **Subject:** and **Date:**. Most companies have a standard printed memorandum form for employees to use.

Since a memorandum is internal your signature is not required, although some people sign informally, or place their initials next to their name.

**Examples of Memorandums**

---

### MEMORANDUM

| TO | All staff |
|------|-----------|
| FROM | George Brown |
| DATE | 18 Feb 19-- |

---

Anyone having holiday time owing from last year should arrange with Personnel to take it before April 1.

---

# MEMORANDUM

TO       ALL STAFF

FROM    J. H. C.   John

21 October 19--

As you may already know, the Directors are considering the possibility of installing a computer to assist us with stock control, order processing and sales ledgers.

At this stage it is still only a possibility and we may yet find that the costs outweigh the benefits. To help us establish the costs involved we are asking a firm of consultants, Jefferson Associates, to produce a system specification for us. One of their staff, Clifford Ongen, will be spending about a week in the office, starting on November 2nd. Others will help him at various times.

Before starting this project, however, we want all our staff to be assured of the following points.

- We have complete confidence in everyone's ability tocontinue to run the present uncomputerised system.
- We are considering introducing a computer system because we are anticipating modest growth in the business and we want to handle such growth without the need to make any alterations to our existing staff.
- If we decide to computerise our systems it will have a significant effect on everyone's work and a thorough training programme will be an integral part of any contract we make with a manufacturer. We are confident of everyone's ability to cope with any changes that are made to our working methods.

The consultants' first task is to observe exactly what we do at present and how we do it. We want them to see a true picture of the company - warts and all! Nobody is being tested. It is not our staff but our systems (and in some areas our lack of them) that are being examined, so please continue with our work as normally as possible while Clifford Ongen or his colleagues are here, and be quite frank and honest when discussing any aspects of our work with them.

I shall be finding an opportunity during the next few days to speak to everyone about our plans. Meanwhile, please contact me if you have any queries.

Example of memorandum on instructions for writing and filing periodic reports.

---

## SIMPSON METALS LTD

To:      J Tompkins
              S Tims
              R James

From:    J Hollingworth           February 15, 199_

Subject:  Monthly Reports

From this month onwards I would like your monthly report to be split into two sections.

Section 1 is to contain the narrative part of your report and should be with me before the end of the month. Section 2 is to contain figures only and should be on my desk no later than a week after section 1.

Section 1 should contain these items:

− National Manufacturing Budgets,
− Promotional Report,
− Gains/Losses on Account Customers,
− Gains/Losses on Developers,
− National Top 40 Customer Analysis,
− Market & Competitive Information,
− Research & Development Report,
− Any Other Information and
− Action for Next Period.

This month, Section 1 of the February report should reach me by February 25, Section 2 by first post 28 February.

---

# 11
## PERIODIC
## REPORTS

Periodic reports are written to indicate that something has been done within a given time.

## —————————— Purpose ——————————

Periodic reports are written and/or published at the same time each hour, day, week, month or year to indicate specified work that has been accomplished, or to indicate the status of something within that time. The annual reports that large corporations issue to indicate what has been accomplished within the past year are a good example of long periodic reports, as are yearly personnel appraisals. On the other hand, a building site manager may fill in the blanks on a form at the end of each day to indicate to the supervisor what has been done that day, or what supplies have been ordered, or which workers have been present.

In a welding shop, for example, a periodic report is written up (usually by filling in blanks on a form) at the end of each hour to indicate exactly what has been done in the shop within that hour. Additional status reports (see pages 184–7) may be written at the end of each day or each week indicating work accomplished on a specific item requiring welding. In this case, the periodic report would indicate to management what has been done within each hour by what employees on what sort of welding. There might also be status reports for the ongoing work on each item sent to the welding shop for repair. All these reports would be filed to form a legal record of work accomplished.

Often a period report appears as spaces on a form to be filled in for each item required. This makes it a relatively easy report to complete.

It may be tempting to stretch the truth on a periodic report to make your work look better. Resist this temptation by remembering that besides the moral issues of dishonesty, you may be held legally liable for the contents of the report.

The following items need to be included in any period report:

(a) the intervals at which it is written;
(b) the time, date and person writing it;
(c) the time between this report and the previous one filed;
(d) the equipment or items covered in it;
(e) the personnel involved in the work;
(f) the action accomplished and names of any people involved;
(g) the signature of the person submitting the report.

# 12

## PROGRESS REPORTS

Progress reports are written at pre-determined intervals to record the state of work accomplished within the determined time. Whereas a periodic report focuses on the state of the shop or the company, a progress report focuses on the state of a particular project or operation.

## Purpose

The purpose of any progress report is to explain exactly what progress has been made within a particular time span. While the status report conveys information about the condition of something that is static the progress report by its very name implies that movement has taken place, that something has changed and that conditions are different from (and let's hope better than) what they were when the last report was submitted.

# Content

A progress report should contain these items:

- a clear statement of the purpose of the particular progress report;
- the name of the person or team involved in the work;
- a clear statement of the subject, including a brief description of it if necessary;
- the current date and length of time since the previous progress report and its date;
- any change in personnel, either the workers or the writer of the report;
- the place where the work was done, or the investigation took place, and any changes in either since the last report;
- the stage the work had reached at the time of last reporting;
- specific measurements about how the work was accomplished, with changes since the previous report, how that work was measured, when and by whom, including all necessary figures;
- what work remains to be done before the project is finished.

Usually the progress report is not long. A page might suffice, although sometimes progress reports can be interim reports written as part of a longer report. If you have a research grant you will probably be required to produce a report at the end detailing the work accomplished, but at stated intervals before that you may be required to write a progress report entitled 'Work to Date'. Consultants often file interim reports on progress to indicate to their clients that they have not been forgotten. (Such reports can sometimes be called *draft reports*.)

Whatever your firm calls its progress reports, try to keep them short and to the point. You would not want your reader to become bogged down in 'progress'.

## Exercise

Think of the last task you were given in the office by a manager and write a short, one-page progress report on what you have actually accomplished on it in the past day, or week. Cover each of the items listed above. Put it aside and read it one week later or whenever you finish the task. See if your report was then an accurate indication of how you had progressed in doing the task.

Here is an example of a Progress Report.

Cleghorn Waring & Co (Pumps) Ltd
Icknield Way
Letchworth, Herts.

Crossman Engineering Co Ltd
85 Richardson Place
Bolton

Attn: Mr Thomas Jackson

<u>Repair of Chester OFI-series pumps</u>

We have received the three pumps you have sent to us and have carried out the following work.

1   Two of the pumps were stripped down and the interiors were found to be dry, with minor wear but no visible damage to the working surfaces of the graphite stator components. The stainless steel rotor surfaces were all extensively rusted, with the vanes locked into the slots. It is not possible to determine whether this corrosion occurred in service or at some time after the pumps were taken out of commission.

2   As swelling of the sintered graphite vanes and stator components had been considered as a possible cause of seizure, the pumps were rebuilt using Graph-met composite vanes and stator components. The rotors were thoroughly cleaned, and the pumps were reassembled and tested. The pumps operated up to standard except for an appreciable drop in the measured flow rate at maximum pressure, which is attributable to rotor wear.

3   The third pump, however, is so corroded that it cannot be stripped down without danger of sustaining further damage. We doubt the value of proceeding further with our investigations and repairs and recommend that you consider buying a replacement pump. The Chester OFI pumps are still obtainable (in stock, £345 + VAT), but you might find that the newer model, Chester ONP (in stock, £462 + VAT), would better suit the harsh conditions in which your pumps must operate.

4   As there was no evidence of faulty workmanship or assembly in the first two pumps, we would not normally consider them for repair under warranty, but we have repaired them free of charge in the interests of goodwill. We are waiting for your instructions on how to proceed with the third pump and are sending you full details about the Chester ONP-style pump.

Regards,

W H Cleghorn

W. H. Cleghorn

# 13

## —— PROPOSALS ——

Any proposal is a statement about future work, work which you hope to obtain, dependent on the specifications presented in the proposal. Thus, it is about ideas and about your ability to present those ideas in clear, easy-to-understand prose for your particular reader.

A proposal focuses on the future, not on the present, on your ideas about improving the future situation in a particular company or organisation. It is your job in the proposal to convince your audience that the ideas should be adopted, can be achieved, are realistic, will improve the company's position or production and can be accomplished at a reasonable cost.

You, the writer, think the idea is excellent, but if you fail to convince your reader then the proposal has failed. Any proposal is successful only to the extent that you are able to convince your audience of your ability to do the work proposed to accomplish the specifications. The proposal is your chance to do this.

# ———— Purpose ————

The purpose of a proposal is to convince your readers that your idea about their future is the only correct once, the one they should purchase, the particular one they need. It is possible that your firm may have additional purposes. Perhaps, for instance, your manager wants you to persuade the readers to buy additional services that they do not yet know they need. If this is part of your brief from your manager then you have a dilemma. You, the writer, have two purposes: one from the client (your audience), and another from your manager (your firm). Make sure you understand both of these purposes thoroughly. Talk to your manager about them.

**It is essential that you never begin writing any proposal without completely understanding its purpose. There is no room or space for deviation from the avowed purpose. If you do deviate you will lose your audience immediately and you may not have another chance.**

# ———— Audience ————

Each proposal is tailor-made for its audience. That is why you are being asked for a proposal. The client you are dealing with has a problem – considered unique, even if you know it is not. He or she wants it addressed individually for the company. Since it is your job to personalise the proposal for the company it is essential that you understand the language the client uses in the conduct of business.

**Remember that the writing is audience-oriented. If it is not the audience will not understand it. Use the readers' language: if the proposal is not understood on the first reading it will not be accepted.**

# Types of proposals

There are different types of proposals depending on the kind of work to be done. One type deals with basic research, especially research for a new product, such as a search for missile paint that will not destruct on re-entering the Earth's atmosphere, or in other high-temperature environments. Another deals with the development of a new product through to the production line. Others can be about planning for development, or for any other aspect of business, such as total quality management. Another type focuses on sales. You could, for example, be asked to develop a new sales plan, or a marketing plan for a new product which is not yet developed.

Sometimes proposals present completely new management structures for firms, or new ways of handling a particular personnel problem. Often a proposal requires that you and your team spend a lot of time deciding how to do the thing required. It takes research on your part to put the proposal together. If there were an easily recognised solution there would, of course, be no need to ask for a proposal in the first place.

A tender is a proposal written in answer to a call for proposals (an invitation to tender), defining the specific job the proposal addresses. The form of the tender is usually specified in the invitation and you should follow this form very carefully. You can count on many other companies submitting tenders (and all the tenders are opened at the same time). What will make your tender stand out is accuracy, thoroughness, originality and a spotless presentation.

Different industries, businesses and governmental agencies may use other names for proposals, but the basic principles for writing them remain the same.

# Content

No matter what the subject of the proposal it must provide answers to the following questions that will be in the minds of your readers:

1   What do you propose to do?
2   How do you propose to do it?
3   What evidence can you present to show that the methods you propose to use will actually get the desired results?
4   What evidence can and should you present to show that your way of obtaining the desired results is better than any other way?
5   How can you demonstrate your ability to do what you propose to do?
6   What evidence must you present to show that the cost will be acceptable and that you can meet a satisfactory time schedule?
7   What personnel do you propose to use to achieve this?
8   What will the end product be: a report, or series of reports? Will there be period, status or progress reports?

Do not start outlining your proposal until you have the answers in full to these questions. Make sure you include any technical descriptions, diagrams, charts, etc. which will help explain your proposals. Then begin to outline. Be creative in your thinking about the outline and what to include and how to get your points across. This is your new idea and you want to present it clearly and in the best possible light. This is a chance to be creative in your presentation as well as in your ideas. You may decide that some sections, such as cost, will be presented at a later stage once the client has accepted the first part.

**Remember: effective proposals require careful thought, both about the content and the structure.**

# The pattern

Before you begin to consider what patterns you want to use think further about your audience. (See pages 9–15.) Who will be reading the proposal? How many of them will be making the decision about whether to approve it? What are their backgrounds? These questions are even more important – if that is possible – when writing a proposal than with any other form of business writing. Since you are writing about an 'idea' with which your readers may not be at all familiar you must write in language that makes them feel comfortable. If possible, read some of their reports and documents before writing to know what sort of tone and style they use. Find out about their backgrounds. Do not talk down to them but, on the other hand, do not use vocabulary they are not going to understand.

Having done this, think again about your material and how you want to present it. Perhaps one of your company's strong points is the experience and background of the personnel who will be working on the project. How do you present them most favourably in the proposal? Do you include mini-biographies of each one? Do you need to stress the experience they have with this sort of project already, or is that risky because the client will then wonder how unique the proposal is? If you are aware that the client has particular prejudices against a type of work area omit that background in the biography of your personnel. In other words, make sure the proposal fits the audience as precisely as you can honestly make it.

After careful consideration outline your proposal, being creative when necessary with various sections of it. Make sure to include at least the following sections:

*(a)*  Cover Sheet/Title Page;
*(b)*  Summary or Abstract (not more than 3 per cent of the total);
*(c)*  Table of Contents, Tables of Charts, Graphs, Illustrations, etc.;
*(d)*  Statement of Request (use this instead of the recommendations section you include in a formal report), which includes Who, What, When and How much;
*(e)*  The Body, which includes a statement of the problem, the background to it, the scope of the proposal, methodology, facilities, personnel advantages and disadvantages, duration of project, costs and reports to be issued during and after the project.

# — How your proposal will be judged —

Your client, the audience, will be using a number of criteria to judge the effectiveness and strengths of your proposal. Some of these you will not know, but others are used for every proposal, by every company. They will include:

- cost;
- performance;
- reliability;
- economy of operation;
- delivery of the product (which may be a report) at the time needed.

Remember that every company is interested in increasing profits and enhancing its reputation. Company members will be judging your proposal solely from their point of view.

Members of international bodies reviewing proposals have explained that writers of proposals must remember that the recommendations any panel makes about the acceptance or rejection of a particular proposal are based only 'on the information in the proposal'. Be sure, therefore, that your proposal covers everything your readers need to know; do not make them guess. The most frequent fault of all proposals is vagueness.

**Remember when writing your proposal that this is your only chance to impress your audience. You will not be there to explain. You must assume that you will not be given another chance. Do not be vague.**

**And never promise anything you cannot deliver!**

Everything else we have discussed about tone, length, editing, proof-reading and production is critical when putting together a proposal. Make sure you leave time to go over it and correct any errors. Make sure it reads and looks as good as you can possibly make it, given the time you have.

## *Checklist*

1   Is what you propose to do and how you will do it perfectly clear?
2   Have you presented enough evidence for this?
3   Have you fully explained your methodology so your audience can understand it at first reading?
4   Have you provided a system or evidence for demonstrating that you can do what you propose?
5   Are the costs and the time schedule clear and reasonable?

**6**  Are all these points very clear in the proposal, especially to someone who knows little or nothing about it?

**7**  Is it easy to read?

**8**  Does it look inviting?

**9**  Have you included all the descriptions, graphs, etc. that might be useful?

(Add your own items to this list.)

# 14

## ———— REFERENCES ————

References are relatively short documents that recommend or refuse to recommend a person or company for a particular job.

Often references are conveyed informally over the telephone, but if there are complications or the person asking for the reference does not know the referee, it is a good idea to have the reference in writing. Another advantage to having a written reference is that it can be filed for future use, perhaps for other jobs or projects.

Usually a reader who calls for references will be in the process of reading many other references, applications and CVs, and it is only considerate to reply promptly and make your reference as clear, concise and direct as you can.

## ———————— Purpose ————————

The purpose of a reference is to provide the reader with enough information to decide whether or not to employ the person or company under discussion. To this end it is essential to be honest. You need not be blunt but, then again, you must not be too vague. It is not helpful to say an employee's attendance 'could have been more regular'; this does not tell your reader very much. Say directly that the employee often missed work. Or better yet, tell your reader that the employee had a pattern of missing work at least once every three weeks and, if possible, state the reasons for the absences.

It is interesting that a reference is one of the very few kinds of business writing where the purpose is almost entirely altruistic. On the face of it, you get nothing in return for your reference. But in the long term a good reference can do your own company a great service. Sending out references can be a form of free advertising. If your reference is well presented, clear and prompt your reader will remember your company and perhaps call upon your services or use your product sometime in the future.

# Content

A good letter asking for a reference will provide questions for you to answer, and so your reference simply answers the questions. (The example below from Euston UK Ltd is obviously structured to answer specific queries from Jason & Son.) Some companies provide a standard form for references, and all you have to do is fill in the pre-determined areas.

There are not many essential ingredients of a letter of reference. Be sure to include the following:
* in what capacity you have known the person or company;
* how long you have known the person or company;
* how reliably and how competently the person or company performed.

# Example of a Reference

EUSTON UK LTD
81–85 BARNLEY ROAD
DUNDEE

Jason & Son Ltd
Parkside Manor
Burnside
Dumfries

28th September 199_
Ref: PVH/ltj

Dear Sir

Thank you for your letter of 20 September, requesting a reference for Clairish Computers Ltd. The answers to your questions are as follows.

1  We have employed Clairish Computers Ltd since January 199_.
2  Clairish Computers has helped our company rectify a new computer system that had been badly installed by another firm of consultants.
    Clairish Computers has drawn up a systems specification for a replacement system and has chosen appropriate hardware.
3  We did not select Clairish Computers from several candidates.
4  We were not first time computer users.
5  Our first system is working satisfactorily. The replacement system is still too new to comment on.
6  We are satisfied with the work of Clairish. The various stages were completed on time, and the charges agreed with the quotes.
7  There was continuity of staff at Clairish Computers. Ian Baird managed the work, which was carried out by Alex Johnston and James MacReady.
8  The staff training was effectively carried out.
9  We would certainly use Clairish again.
10 There was total involvement by Clairish staff, who approached the problem with the same urgency and commitment and sense of practicality expected from an in-house computer team.

Yours faithfully,

Peter Haddon

Peter Haddon, <u>Director</u>

# 15

## STATUS
## REPORTS

A status report describes a current situation or condition. It talks about what exists now, not about any progress or change that is taking place or has taken place. Often a status report will be filed in the middle of a job, at the end of a budgetary period or at a change in shifts.

The contents of a status report always cover the same items that have been covered in previous status reports, e. g. parts of equipment, actions of staff, inventories of supplies or combinations of these.

## Purpose

The purpose of the report is always to inform people of the position, situation or state at that time. It does not mean that progress has necessarily been made since the last report.

**It is the number and accuracy of your details that will produce a useful status report.**

# Content

An adequate status report should cover these items:
- the period of time covered by the report;
- the machinery, supplies, equipment or staff used;
- the location of each of these items;
- the degree of importance of each of these items;
- the precise condition of the items reported on;
- the specific time and place the report was filed;
- the reader/readers of the report and the purpose for reading the report;
- the actions to be taken after reading the report;
- the writer's authorisation.

# The pattern

Since most status reports consist of filling in blank forms, all you have to worry about is inserting the right details into the spaces provided. Occasionally, however, you must write a status report from scratch. If so, follow these general guidelines in this order, unless otherwise directed.

1  *State* the item(s) involved, the time period covered, the time at which you noted the condition and your authorisation.

2  *Describe* the condition, including details of colour, weight, number, size, etc. (Remember to include anything that has changed since the last status report.) If there are many details use separate paragraphs for each.

3  *Add* any further details which you have been asked to include, such as the ranking of importance of the items you have described.

4  *Sign* your name clearly with the time, place and date of submitting the report.

Try to keep the report within three pages. The report could be longer if, for instance, you were reporting on the status of a year-long research project.

**This report constitutes a legal document on the condition of something at a particular time and place. Make sure all the details are accurate.**

### Exercise

Write a short one-page status report on the last job you completed in your company/office as if you were still in the middle of the work.

## Visit reports

One common type of status report is the visit report, in which a sales representative states the prospects for doing business with a regular or potential customer. It might also be a report on a visit to a subsidiary company. Another visit report might be produced by an investigative team about the conditions at a particular site. This kind of report might later be included in a larger report about the site.

Because a visit report often remains in-house, writers may be tempted to leave it in the form of notes. Such a report can quickly become useless if it has to be read by someone else in the company who cannot understand the notes or finds them ambiguous. It is worth taking the extra time to write a clear and direct document that any potential reader can understand.

Example of a Visit Report

---

To:     HKL – NGV – OJT
From:   MMR

### VISIT REPORT

Underjack Technology Ltd                    Mike Hughes
19 Buntingdon Road
Totnes, Devon

Date seen: 10 June 199_

We have quoted Mike Hughes for one large and several small
Masterwell jobs, so far without success. He turns out to be a
one-man band working from home, experienced and well
connected in the business – 17 years with Madison Clark Ltd,
followed by several as an independent consultant and agent.

He must be past 60, and he will probably retire before long.
Interesting and useful to talk to, potentially a customer but
without an organisation to back him, he is not likely to be the
man to promote Masterwell in the South Western region.

---

# 16

## TECHNICAL DESCRIPTIONS

A technical description of something provides an objective, completely factual view of an object, such as a piece of machinery, a factory or a tool. It is often used as part of a longer document, such as a feasibility study, a long report or an environmental impact statement. A technical description tells you what something is, what it looks like, what its function is and what its place is in the scheme of a larger procedure or machine. It does not tell you how to use it or put it together. It is not a process analysis. (See pages 50–4.)

## Purpose

The purpose of a technical description is to provide the reader with a clear-cut, accurate picture of something which will enable the reader to assess or to judge possibilities, to understand what something is so that it can be used, assembled, repaired or assessed.

# Types

There are not many different types of technical description, but different professions would include different specifications in their technical descriptions. Obviously, certain professions such as engineering, architecture, electronics and urban planning would make more use of drawings in their descriptions than other professions.

An architectural company would include a technical description of a site when it was proposing how to build a new office complex on a particular parcel of land within a city. Such a description would include a drawing of the site with buildings marked out and entrances and exits shown, etc. An electrical engineer, on the other hand, would probably use fewer words but include more drawings of plans for the electrical wiring in the new office complex.

# Content

The most important thing about the content of a technical description is to make sure that your facts are absolutely accurate and precise. This is not the time to have fuzzy notions of the size or shape of your object. Measure with an accurate rule; obtain precise details from the manufacturers; double check with any assistants who may be giving you figures.

Think next about the most logical way to describe your object. Look at it from the reader's point of view. What is the reader going to be doing with your description? Think again about the purpose. Will the reader be assembling something, installing equipment, repairing it, using it or training staff how to use it? What is it that they need to know about the object first? What is most important to them in what they are going to be doing with or to it?

Look at two different possible technical descriptions of a desk designed for use in classrooms. The designer must describe the desk so that the production department can order material and plan an operating procedure. This description will specify the exact materials to be used, and their size and shape; it will show every little nut and bolt; it will indicate which parts needed glueing and what kind of glue is required.

There will be another description produced by the marketing department to go out to heads, governors or local authorities who need to know about the desks before they buy them. This description will ignore the nuts and bolts and mention only the major materials, focusing on how durable and practical they are. It will describe the size of the desks (perhaps specifying what age of student they would suit) and may discuss how easily the desks can be moved or stored.

Knowing the audience and purpose will determine the view from which you describe the object and what you say about it, but the following items ought to be covered in any technical description.

1   Describe the whole object without taking any of it apart.

2   Define where it will be used, who will use it, what it will be a part of.

3   State its function either on its own or as part of a larger operation. But do not give step-by-step instructions in how to use it; remember this is not a process analysis.

4   List the parts, or at least those that you are concerned with for your present purpose.

5   Take it apart piece by piece, or put it together if that is the best way to see the object. Do this either:
              inside out or outside in;
              top to bottom or bottom to top;
              from one side or the other;
              as it should be assembled.

**6** Include whatever drawings or schematics are needed to show adequately what it is. Make sure they match the point of view taken in number **5**.

**7** Sum up the description in a conclusion that ties it together with some other operation used with it or after it.

**Remember that a technical description is not emotional but factual and objective. You want to see exactly what is there. It is not a literary description in which you want the 'feelings' evoked by the object. A technical description is not the place for feelings.**

Example of a Technical Description

## CLEGHORN WARING'S REIMA TURBINE PUMPS

The low flow and high pressure characteristics of Cleghorn Waring's Reima turbine pumps are achieved with the aid of a special design of pump rotor.

The patented multi-step rotor has alternate long and short fluid cavities machined into its outer edge. These are profiled to progressively increase the pressure of liquid circulating in the lateral ring channel. This imparts regenerative pressure to the flow towards the discharge port.

Previously, the only way to achieve such performance would have been by using more complex multi-stage centrifugal or high speed gear-driven pump designs.

Capable of producing pulsation free flows from 2 to 72m$^3$/h at heads up to 1400 metres when running at a standard speed of 2900 rev/min, the pump is produced with six basic outer castings, ten standard shafts and four bearing frames to cater for the entire 90-model range.

# INDEX

# Notes

# Notes

# Notes

# THE OFFICE HANDBOOK

## VERA AND CHRISTINA HUGHES

The ideal reference source for the modern office, this book contains an enormously wide range of facts and hints on every aspect of secretarial and clerical work, including:

Communication
The electronic office
Health and safety at work
Legal matters
Meetings and conferences
Money, banking and finance
Organisations
Stationery
Trading documents and procedures
Travel

This compact, concise and convenient handbook is an invaluable desktop companion for all secretarial students and office workers dealing with the day-to-day demands of office life.

TEACH YOURSELF BOOKS

## OTHER TITLES AVAILABLE
## IN TEACH YOURSELF

☐ 0 340 55644 7 **WORD PROCESSING** £4.99
*Vera Hughes*

☐ 0 340 41763 3 **THE OFFICE HANDBOOK** £4.99
*Vera and Christina Hughes*

☐ 0 340 56825 9 **BUSINESS STUDIES** £5.99
*Peter Fearns*

☐ 0 340 58603 6 **COMPANY LAW** £12.99
*Colin Thomas*

*All these books are available at your local bookshop or newsagent, or can be ordered direct from the publisher. Just tick the titles you want and fill in the form below.*

Prices and availability subject to change without notice.

HODDER AND STOUGHTON PAPERBACKS, P.O. Box 11, Falmouth, Cornwall.

Please send cheque or postal order for the value of the book, and add the following for postage and packing:

UK including BFPO – £1.00 for one book, plus 50p for the second book, and 30p for each additional book ordered up to a £3.00 maximum.

OVERSEAS, INCLUDING EIRE – £2.00 for the first book, plus £1.00 for the second book, and 50p for each additional book ordered.

OR Please debit this amount from my Access/Visa Card (delete as appropriate).

CARD NUMBER ☐☐☐☐☐☐☐☐☐☐☐☐☐☐☐☐☐☐

AMOUNT £ . . . . . . . . . . . . . . .

EXPIRY DATE . . . . . . . . . . . . . . .

SIGNED . . . . . . . . . . . . . . . . . . . . . . . . .

NAME . . . . . . . . . . . . . . . . . . . . . . . . . . . . . . . . . . . . . . . . . . . . . . . . . . . . . . . . . .

ADDRESS . . . . . . . . . . . . . . . . . . . . . . . . . . . . . . . . . . . . . . . . . . . . . . . . . . . . . . . .

. . . . . . . . . . . . . . . . . . . . . . . . . . . . . . . . . . . . . . . . . . . . . . . . . . . . . . . . . . . . . . . .